GROWING UP IN THE D

My Grandfather,
My Mother, and Me

CYNTHIA WILLIAMS

ISBN: 1482742772
ISBN-13: 9781482742770

Library of Congress Control Number: 2013905081
CreateSpace Independent Publishing Platform
North Charleston, South Carolina

CONTENTS

ABOUT THE AUTHOR

Cynthia was born and raised in Detroit, Michigan. After graduating from Eastern Michigan University with a master's degree in counseling, she moved to Northville, Michigan, where she has worked in counseling and therapy for over twenty-seven years. She currently resides in Northville. This is her first book.

Cynthia is a recipient of the 2014 Ford Motor Company, Ford Freedom Award. The Freedom Award celebrates those who have demonstrated the power of perseverance and their unwavering commitment to their community.

ABOUT THE PHOTOGRAPHER

Alan Deneau is a national award-winning photojournalist. Alan began his career in photojournalism in 1953 at the age of seventeen in Kalamazoo, Michigan. In 1956, Alan began working full-time for *The Detroit News*. By 1958, Alan won an award for photojournalism in *Look* magazine. By the age of thirty-three, Alan had won over fifty awards as a still cameraman, stemming from his early career at *The Detroit News*. During the civil rights freedom parade down Woodward Avenue on June 23, 1963, Alan covered the story admirably. The photos Alan took of Dr. Martin Luther King Jr. were on the front page of *The Detroit News* that day. Later in 1963, Alan provided film coverage of the death of Dr. LeRoy Augenstein, a prominent scientist and politician. The story was rated one of the top ten in the state by the Associated Press editors. When wreckage of Dr. Augenstein's twin-engine plane was discovered, Alan and his team rushed by car to shoot scenes of the crash area. Alan got one particularly dramatic shot by stepping back into the darkness to capture the search party silhouetted against the wreckage. The film was combined with other interviews and used as an extended report on Dr. Augenstein's untimely death and its probable effect on the state of Michigan. In addition, Alan shot thousands of feet of film that were used in a half-hour show on the St. Lawrence Seaway–Great Lakes system. Alan spent days shooting points on the seaway from the air and on the ground, from the port of Detroit to the Straits of Mackinaw and the Soo Locks in the Upper Peninsula. The final result was "The Fourth Seacoast," the most comprehensive pictorial report ever compiled on the subject for Detroit commercial TV. Alan came to WWJ-TV in 1964 and won at least one award each year for his work as a newsreel cameraman. Alan exhibited both versatility and virtuosity in covering the news in 1969. He was the type of cameraman who kept filming the action during the October antiwar demonstrations even though he and his soundman were being clubbed by police riot sticks. Fortunately, Alan was not hurt. A similar incident occurred early in 1970 when John Norman Collins, on the way to his pretrial hearing in Ann Arbor, shoved Alan's camera into his face. Alan kept filming, despite the minor pain. In 1971, Alan joined WXYZ-Channel 7 News. He was the type of cameraman often called upon to go after the tough assignments, and often the documentary reports required weeks of work.

◆

ACKNOWLEDGMENTS

I am especially indebted to Sylvie Puech and Alan Deneau, who have provided me with the direction and confidence to pursue my dream of writing my story.

Sylvie Puech has been an editor, organizer, interpreter, communications professional, and advisor for the layout of the book. Sylvie's enthusiasm and integrity have been great motivators to me. Her passion made writing my story exciting and provided me with a great feeling of accomplishment.

I am wholeheartedly grateful to Alan Deneau for the use of his beautiful photographs, for his tremendous energy, and dynamic personality. Throughout the writing process, Alan encouraged me to write my story from the heart.

A special thank you goes out to my friend, Bonnie King, who was readily available to offer her wisdom, advice, and compassion on this journey.

I appreciate all of the professional assistance with photo editing that Alek Przybylo provided.

I want to express my heartfelt appreciation to Stacey Reynolds, MLIS in library and information science and author of *Images of America: Flat Rock, Michigan*. Stacey provided copy and developmental editing along with historic research and fact-checking. I am very thankful for her contribution to organizing and enhancing this book. Stacey provided me with tireless guidance and confidence throughout the developmental process.

My deepest thanks to Barbara Bloom for her editing contribution to this book.

All photos in this book are courtesy of Alan Deneau, Stacey Reynolds, or part of my collection. The excerpt from *The Corner: A Century of Memories at Michigan and Trumbull* is printed with permission of Triumph Books. The excerpt from *The Gods of Olympia Stadium: Legends of the Detroit Red Wings* is printed with permission of Richard Kincaide. The excerpts from *The Michigan Central Railroad: History of the Main Line 1846–1901 are* printed with permission from Nicholas A. Marsh.

PREFACE

My intention in writing this memoir is to inspire others to come to the understanding that even if they have only one adult in their life who is nurturing and stable, that presence can lift them up and out of whatever difficult place they find themselves, in a powerful and reparative way.

This is a true story based on the strong emotional bonds I developed as a child with my paternal grandfather, Robert, and in a peculiar way with my mother, June. As far back as I can recall, I remember my parents' ongoing struggle—their inability to meet a child's needs or maintain, what I thought at the time was, a "normal" home. I learned not only about determination and love from my grandfather, Robert, but also about being emotionally, intellectually, and spiritually disciplined. I am writing this book as a tribute to my grandfather and to acknowledge the great personal sacrifices and struggles he lived through so that I could sustain some semblance of normalcy within our family. I am also writing this memoir as a testament of my early life living with a parent with mental health issues, the trauma that I experienced that was often overlooked, and how through the close, sustained relationship with my grandfather I developed the characteristics of other resilient children.

I began writing this book with humility and a sense of purpose, and it seems to have taken on a life of its own. I found myself writing every evening after returning home from my full-time position as a therapist. I work with children and adolescents who have also experienced trauma at some point in their lives. Night after night, I sat at my little oak desk, which I purchased many years ago, and typed late into the evening.

When I first began to write this book, it was not obvious to me that it would be so cathartic. I went through a transformation, and as time went by, I became determined to complete this book. I am convinced that readers can draw strength from it and that it can touch others in a powerful and profound way.

This memoir looks through a nostalgic lens and captures some historic times in Detroit as remembered by Robert and Lillian Williams (my paternal grandparents), my parents, and me. Growing up in Detroit during the 1950s and 1960s, I personally witnessed the advent of the civil rights movement. As I rode the public bus from Northwest Detroit into the inner city to see the beauty of Christmas at Hudson's, it resonated in my soul to see so many young African American men and women living in impoverished neighborhoods. I saw the surge of energy and industry in Detroit as it became the automobile capital of the world and the lure of the Ford Rotunda with its cars of the future. I experienced the excitement and wild emotion of the Olympia Stadium as it attracted renowned musicians, like the Beatles, from all over the world.

I remember the thrill of taking the Boblo boat to Boblo Island and recall looking up in wonder at the massive

Ambassador Bridge as the boat slowly traveled underneath it. I remember the Detroit Tigers playing ball at Briggs Stadium and listening to the powerful voice of Ernie Harwell as they transformed an ordinary summer day into an event that the people of Detroit felt passionate about.

During this time, Detroit local television produced shows such as *The Soupy Sales Show, Milky's Party Time* presented by Twin Pines Dairy, *The Johnny Ginger Show,* and *Rita Bell Prize Movie.* My favorite show was *The Soupy Sales Show,* and I proudly wore my Soupy Sales dress with a red-and-white bow tie as I laughed out loud watching Soupy get smacked in the face with a cream pie on a daily basis. I recall spending many hours watching programs, such as *John Cameron Swayze, The Ed Sullivan Show, The Lawrence Welk Show, The Linkletter Show, The Lou Gordon Show, Leave It to Beaver, The Twilight Zone, Lassie, The Jack Benny Program,* and *Alfred Hitchcock Presents* on a black-and-white TV at my grandparents' home on Archdale Street. Also at this time, Detroit radio stations were playing Motown Records hits, such as "Dancing in the Street" by Martha and the Vandellas and "Where Did Our Love Go?" by the Supremes.

I think of my grandfather every day. Although the struggles and challenges I encountered as a child are far behind me, I believe my grandfather's faith, love, determination, perseverance, and courage remain within me. In my time here on earth and in my time spent with my grandfather, I have come to fully understand the meaning of unfailing love. I have seen what a truly disciplined person looks like. I have learned that without holding on tightly to our faith, we walk in peril and fear.

During my youth I made the best of the situation with my parents and was deeply grateful for my grandfather and his determination to meet the challenges my older brother and later, my younger sister and I presented to him. My grandfather was a reassuring presence each time he visited our home, and I could count on his unfailing love for me time after time, as each crisis unfolded. Throughout my youth, I could turn to my grandfather and learned to rely on him as I sought to overcome challenges, sorrow and setbacks. With each obstacle I faced, I became more determined to face them with renewed faith and took the steps necessary to live a life with balance and joy in it.

CHAPTER 1

THE EARLY YEARS

Continuous effort-not strength or intelligence-is the key to unlocking our potential.

—Sir Winston Churchill (1874-1965)

Love Was the Cornerstone

My paternal grandfather, Robert Frederick Williams, was born September 19, 1886 in Detroit, Michigan. He grew up in a world that was stable, loving and with old-fashioned values. In 1886, Detroit was a thriving city of about 133,000 people. Baseball in Detroit dates back to 1859. It was considered to be a gentlemen's sport well into the late 1800s. Not surprisingly, baseball with its vitality and unbounded energy became even more popular after the American Civil War.

During the summer of 1886, at Recreation Park, horse-drawn carriages would hold early baseball fans as they watched the Detroit team play against Chicago. Recreation

Park is where the first major league game was played and it was located at Brady Street and Alexanderine Avenue East.

The Detroit team took the name of the Detroit Tigers when they entered the American League in 1901. By April, 1901, the Detroit Tigers played baseball at Bennett Park with 10,000 fans watching. Bennett Park was located at the corner of Michigan Avenue and Trumbull. The Detroit Tigers would go on to play there for another ninety-eight years.

In January, 1886, the building of the Michigan Central railway was well underway. Detroit became known as the primary center that hid thousands of African American families as they made their way to freedom from the south. The families were hidden in remote and unknown places in Detroit and Ann Arbor. As difficult as it was for the families to remain concealed, many of the employees of the Michigan Central railway deliberately ensured that they were.

My grandfather, Robert, learned the virtues of hard work, compassion, courage, and faith from a very young age. These virtues were instilled within me as a child growing up in Detroit.

My grandfather's parents were born in Wales, England and immigrated to Stratford, Ontario, Canada, and then moved to Windsor, Ontario, where they lived for a short time. In 1885, my grandfather's father served in the Twenty-First Regiment in Canada. By 1886, my paternal great-grandparents moved to Detroit to start their family. At that time, my great-grandfather, Frederick Thomas Williams, began working for Michigan Central Railroad (later to become part of the New York

Central) and in a short period of time was promoted to the position of supervisor. Sarah, my paternal great-grandmother was a strong-willed, outspoken person, with a heavy Welsh accent who loved classic literature. According to my grandfather, Sarah had a very positive and close relationship with him. You could say she relied on him and he proved to be a reliable and dutiful son as he met with misfortune and tragedy.

The Williams' Arrive in Detroit

With a twinkle in his eyes, my grandfather would often reflect on memories from his childhood and share them with me. Robert came from humble beginnings and his first home in Detroit was a modest house with no electricity or plumbing. There was an outhouse in the back, and within arm's reach, the Sears catalog that was used for toilet paper.

Back then, the only refrigeration available was a small ice box that held a large block of ice, which was replaced every three days. In Detroit, the ice was delivered by a horse and wagon that came from a source called an underground storage room. Originally the ice was cut from the lakes in Michigan during the winter months and shipped by trains to the city, where it was then distributed to homes. Robert once described how people in his youth would have to eat salt pork because fresh meat and refrigeration were not always available. The meat was cut up, cooked, and stored in barrels of salt. My grandfather recalled how eating too much of this pork would result in painful boils on the skin that would have to be lanced. Despite the possible boils, my grandfather enjoyed the dish and continued to eat pickled pigs' feet throughout his life, which were a reminder to him of those old salt pork days.

During the long winter months, the wind could be heard howling outside the drafty windows. Inside the house, the family used candles and lanterns for light. Robert was seven years old when Edison patented his first successful light bulb. He said the family had one bathtub, which was used twice a week for a bath. It was filled just once each time. He stressed the point that no one wanted to be the last one to take a bath!

His mother, Sarah, was a source of strength and great compassion for him as he grew up in Detroit. Sarah encouraged Robert to read his Bible every evening and then engaged him in a discussion about what he read. Sarah taught Robert manners and how to treat a lady with respect. Every year at Christmas, throughout his boyhood, my great-grandparents placed small, white candles in a holder for lights on the Christmas tree. They had to keep a vigilant watch so that a fire did not break out. A full English breakfast was promptly served by six o'clock Christmas morning, and the entire family attended the First Presbyterian Church on Woodward Avenue in Detroit. As a child, Robert was not overindulged and Christmas gifts usually were practical items like knitted hats and scarves.

During the late 1880s and into the beginning of the twentieth century, when my grandfather was a young man, he witnessed the advent of the automotive age, the early years of baseball, the electric streetcar system, the phenomenon of electricity, the first successful aircraft, improvements to the telephone, the exciting transition from steam-powered train engines to gasoline locomotives and the civil rights movement.

Off to Work

My grandfather had little time for relaxation. If he had any spare time, he grabbed his fishing pole and ran to the nearest pond where he found some quiet time to think. My grandfather's first paying job was at the age of eleven. He would arrive every morning at five o'clock at a local dairy. He would hitch a horse to a delivery wagon and drive carefully through the dirt streets of Detroit to deliver milk. Once he was done with his deliveries, he would then head directly to school. My grandfather had to help the family, and it was a common occurrence for children to attend school until the eighth grade and then go on to work full-time. In 1899 when Robert was thirteen years old, Henry Ford built his first auto factory in Highland Park, Michigan. Robert revealed that during the nighttime he could hear the far-off whistle of a train and dreamed of working for the railroad, spending his days as part of a crew that made long journeys to cities in Michigan to pick up resources for the emerging Industrial Age. Marsh (*Michigan Central Railroad*, 103,105, and 203) states:

> *The first Detroit station house was built or purchased by the state prior to 1838. It was a one-story, wooden structure that served both passenger and freight business and was located at the intersection of Woodward and Fort Streets in Detroit at Campus Martius. In 1848 the MCRR shifted the Main Line toward the river and built a new depot on Third Street between River Street (later known as Woodbridge Street and later Jefferson Avenue). This is now roughly the present location of Joe Louis Arena and the Detroit River. It remained in service as a warehouse for years*

after a newer depot was built in 1883. The last depot at this location was at the corner of Third and Woodbridge streets, and operated until the upper story and clock tower burned in 1913. It was replaced by the great Michigan Central Station on Vernor Ave. and 16th St. near Michigan Ave.

What is particularly interesting about the Michigan Central Railroad and its history is the connection to the Underground Railroad and the abolitionists. Marsh goes on to state:

The Underground Railroad was the name given to the loosely organized group of individuals who helped fugitive slaves escape from bondage during pre-Civil War days. These individuals belonged to, or sympathized with, abolitionist organizations. It was during abolitionist meetings that the networks were formed, which laid the track on the Underground Railroad system. The role of the operator, or conductor, as they were usually called, was to pass fugitive slaves from town to town, often along an existing railway, until they were safely out of southern slave hunters' reach.

Without the assistance from the conductor, the slaves would not have escaped to freedom through Michigan. Marsh states: *The MCRR's role in transporting slaves was a secret known by Underground Railroad conductors. The Fugitive Slave Law of 1837 made it illegal for anyone to interfere with a master's right to his slave property, but the law was weak and contemptible to antislavery sympathizers.*

My great-grandfather, Frederick, often spoke of the Michigan Central legacy of hiring African Americans well into the late 1800s and beyond. Marsh concludes, *"One can only speculate how the MCRR became involved in the Underground Railroad and how they stayed out of legal trouble with federal authorities. Perhaps the company had a do not ask and do not tell policy of its own—we don't ask how you are using our trains to smuggle slaves and don't you tell anyone if you do."*

During my childhood days spent with my grandfather, he told me of the lazy summer days of his youth. Robert would often take the time to listen to the sounds of bull frogs croaking, birds chirping, and bees buzzing, or he would notice the splashing of small fish in a river that wound through the forest behind his home. One sweltering summer day when he was fourteen, Robert lay with a friend in a tall, grassy field behind his house. The sun was brilliant, the air was hot, and he could hear the sound of the grass rustling; the scent of lavender filled the air. He relaxed there for some time, memorizing the shapes of the clouds, with his arms folded behind his head, smoking corn silk. I imagine he would have been thinking this was acceptable because his friend introduced it to him and he had seen other boys his age smoking it. Suddenly, when he thought he was secluded, to his embarrassment and great fear, he was discovered by his father and consequently got a whipping for smoking the corn silk. He shed many tears that night and for the first time began to develop a sense of control over his actions.

In just four years, one of his childhood dreams came through. In 1901, at age fifteen, Robert began working full time for the Michigan Central Railroad riding train cars to Port Huron and back to Detroit six days a week. Robert started out working in the steam engine room, shoveling coal into the massive locomotive engine, even in summer with temperatures well into the 90s and 100s. He even learned to walk on top of all the cars while the train was in full motion.

Eight years later, Robert worked his way up to a steam locomotive driver. The work had been satisfying and it was all he had dreamed about. He was responsible for the starting, stopping and the speed of the locomotive. On the long train rides he spent time listening to stories from the older, more experienced railroad men. The railroad men talked about the many train wrecks that had occurred around the turn of the century and the fact that they were now becoming a part of the past. My grandfather never tired of sounding the whistle during the thousands of railroad crossings to give a warning of the train's arrival throughout Michigan. As the train made its way through towns, villages and cities, stopping briefly at many depots or overnight, Robert soon discovered a new world of people very different from himself and his small circle of family and friends in Detroit. As the railroad line stretched out ahead of him, he looked out the window from the engine of the train, and he felt invigorated by the power and demands his job provided. In his new world, Robert became aware of the beauty and simplicity surrounding him, he fell in love and decided there was no place else he would rather be. Robert did not serve in World War I as he was working at that time on the railroad and the government needed highly qualified trainmen.

ROBERT (FIFTH FROM THE LEFT),
circa 1905 (AUTHOR'S COLLECTION)

A Twist of Fate

In 1909, Robert's father, Frederick, a supervisor, was also working at the main Detroit yard. My grandfather said that working any job on the railroad during this time of the century was extremely dangerous. One beautiful spring day in May on the way to work, my grandfather and Frederick both laughed about waking up late that morning because they were up late talking about improvements needed in operations along the Michigan Central Railroad line. My grandfather arrived at the Detroit yard with his father, Frederick. Shortly after he began working that morning, Frederick expressed concern to his workers because two men in his crew did not show up for work. The two men had an unstable work history, which amounted to being suspended for missing work and spending their workday at the local bar. This placed Frederick in a precarious situation and immediately it became necessary for him to run up ahead of the remainder of his crew and position a freight train near the switch. Frederick was waiting to turn the switch just as another freight train was approaching and he did not see it. He desperately grabbed at a handle that was on the switch. It was too late. He was standing dangerously close, which resulted in him getting crushed. This would be just the beginning of more than one occasion when my grandfather had to face death. My grandfather ran to the horrible scene and was suddenly consumed by deep darkness and loneliness. Frederick was a great source of strength for my grandfather. After his father's death, Robert kept the ring Frederick had been wearing when he died, which showed the break in the band from the accident. My grandfather gave no thought to abandoning the railroad. He became even more determined to continue working for the railroad just as his father had for so long, and chose to focus on all the ways his father learned to persevere through a deep abiding faith in God.

In another twist of fate, that same year grandfather started dating Lillian E. Sumner. Lillian was born October 20, 1884, in Ann Arbor, Michigan. Lillian grew up on a farm in Ann Arbor and was one of seven children. She went to Stone School, a one-room schoolhouse, which is still standing to this day. In 1902, Lillian attended Cleary College, located in Ypsilanti, Michigan, and in two years completed business classes, including accounting. By 1905, Lillian had secured a position as a buyer with the J.L. Hudson Company and lived in a boarding house next door to Sarah, my grandfather's sister, my grandfather Robert and his mother, Sarah (my paternal great-grandmother). Sarah introduced Lillian to Robert, and over time Lillian and Robert became best friends.

Society's rules back then were very strict and couples were vigilant in following them. As my grandfather told it, beginning in 1909 they dated for four years and for all of those years they were platonic friends. My grandfather was always a gentleman and would walk my grandmother home after every date, kiss her hand and then say, "Goodnight, my dear!"

ROBERT F. WILLIAMS   (AUTHOR'S COLLECTION)   LILLIAN E. WILLIAMS

Love and Exhilaration

My grandfather said some family members raised their eyebrows because of the age difference between my grandfather and grandmother. Robert was twenty-seven years old and Lillian was twenty-nine years old when they were married. Marriage was a serious enterprise, and they had saved a large amount of money so they could go on an unforgettable honeymoon to Yellowstone National Park. They traveled by train and stage coach to experience the overwhelming beauty and vastness of the wild Wyoming skies in 1914.

Excited to go on their first long trip together to see what the Wild West was like, they arrived at the Michigan Central Station in Detroit. Robert recalled that the Station came alive on that clear, crisp September morning, as they walked through the immense station to the ticket window. The dark mahogany benches were noticeable along with the huge, prominent clock above the entranceway to where the trains waited to be boarded. There was a young man, maybe thirteen years old, with dark brown hair, wearing a brown tweed cap and brown knickers with red suspenders, hard at work shining men's shoes as they sat up high on red chairs and smoked cigars. Men's voices echoed destinations through the station and Robert pulled out his silver pocket watch with roman numerals on it to make sure they were not late for their train. In the midst of the excitement of being in love and traveling to a far-off place, they did not hear the distant sound of the whistle of a Michigan Central train slowly making its way into the station to be reloaded with coal and then to proceed onward so they could commence with their long journey together out West. My grandfather was caught up in the romance and adventure of this time in history, visibly moved by streams of people hurrying to catch trains that would take them to destinations that up until now had not been accessible. For a moment he was a part of their laughter, their loud voices and high energy as they moved swiftly past him. He suddenly realized he would have to run with his new bride to locate the train car they needed to board. Once at the train car, my grandparents waited patiently to board the dark green train with red window frames. Robert was a handsome man, with a full head of dark brown hair, a prominent English nose, and piercing brown eyes. He wore a black suit, a black vest, a starched white shirt with a red silk tie, a black fedora hat, and shiny black shoes and felt nervous about the long train ride and departure from the familiarity of the city. There were a few people already on the train, looking out of the windows at the passengers waiting to board. Many of the women wore large, colorful hats with plumes and high, buttoned-up dresses that were the style in the early twentieth century. The men sitting across from the women had serious expressions on their faces and any harsh sounds seemed to annoy them. They wore dark tweed suits, heavily starched white high neck shirts, colorful narrow silk ties, a dark vest, a pocket watch that was checked periodically and a black derby.

Lillian was elegant, confident and calm. She wore a long beige linen dress, beige button-up shoes, a crisp white cotton shirt that buttoned all the way to the top and a gold photo pin on her suit jacket. Her auburn hair was upswept with a white hair barrette in back and a velvet dark brown hat with a purple plume in the back.

Robert considered Lillian intellectually superior to himself in some ways. After all, she had attended business school, while he had only completed the eighth grade. Still, it did not matter because my grandfather had married his best friend. They were caught up in each other. Their conversation held euphoria about it and they talked about everything they hoped to see, their trip itinerary and their plans for the future.

The powerful steam locomotive sped toward its destination, passing the tall, dry cornfields, farms, covered bridges, winding rivers, lakes and streams as the whistle echoed throughout the night. Robert and Lillian were enveloped in the ever-changing landscape speaking to each other only in hushed tones. It was peaceful as the view from the train changed from day to night. My grandparents were surrounded by the beauty of the immense wilderness and realized this was an once-in-a-lifetime journey.

After an unforgettable five-day trip by train and stagecoach, they reached Old House. Old House was built in 1904 and is the original part of the Old Faithful Inn, which is now a national historic landmark. This historic log-and-wood-shingle, rustic-style lodge sits adjacent to the magnificent Old Faithful geyser. My grandparents sat on the immense front porch and watched Old Faithful erupt in full view. It was incredible, their eyes rising to catch a glimpse of one of nature and God's greatest creations. The rest of the world faded away as they became one with the infinite beauty in front of them. They felt the slow steady pounding of the geyser, the mist on their faces; they observed the cobalt blue sky in the background, the spiritual quietness, and the cool air. In *The National Parks: America's Best Idea*, Ken Burns and Dayton Duncan write:

> *The U.S. Army had been sent into Yellowstone in 1886 on a stop-gap basis, when Congress—frustrated by a series of incompetent and occasionally corrupt civilian superintendents—had simply refused to appropriate any money to oversee it. Up to four troops of cavalry were stationed at the newly constructed Fort Yellowstone, near the Mammoth Hot Springs. They patrolled the sprawling two million acres of park on horseback, doing their best to enforce improvised regulations against poaching, vandalism, and negligence with campfires. The cavalry was also in charge of the nation's three other national parks—Yosemite, General Grant, and Sequoia, all in California. Some of them were African Americans—the celebrated Buffalo Soldiers who had made a name for themselves in the Indian wars. Their commander was Captain Charles Young, born into slavery in Kentucky, whose father had escaped bondage during the Civil War to enlist in the Union army. As superintendent of Sequoia, Young directed his men to complete the first wagon road into the Giant Forest. They accomplished more in one summer than had been done in the three previous years combined. His troops adored him. "He was a father, brother, teacher and a real true friend at all times under all conditions," one of his men remembered, "I really loved him."*

After returning from their honeymoon, they built their two-story brick flat on Dailey Avenue in Detroit. It was completed in 1914. Like many of the other large homes on the street, the upstairs was rented out as a second income. My grandparents befriended a Jewish family, who lived upstairs from them from the 1930s through the 1950s. On many occasions, Mrs. Kaufman would have a sizzling steak waiting for my grandfather when he arrived home after working a long shift for the railroad. In the basement, there was a workbench and tools where, in 1951, my grandfather made my brother, Jim, a wooden toy freighter. Great Lakes freighters were a common sight on the Detroit River for over a hundred years and carried iron ore from Wisconsin, Minnesota and the Upper Peninsula of Michigan to Detroit.

Tragedies and Faith

Tragedies are not unique to this time period. Sadly, my grandfather was not immune to these events. In addition to his father's tragic death, he also recalled the death of his young sister, Emma, a toddler who died of pneumonia. During the early 1900s, an influenza pandemic affected the entire world, especially people between the ages of fifteen and thirty-four. In 1918, when my grandfather was thirty-two years old, his sister, Sarah, died at the age of nineteen, from influenza. Remembering those times, he remarked how a person would be healthy one day and the next day would be afflicted with the influenza and die. Sarah's death had a devastating effect on my grandfather. He often talked about Sarah with a faraway look and tears in his eyes. There were two Sarah's in my grandfather's life, and now, one was gone. All he had now were beautiful memories of the sister he could share anything with.

Spiritually, I believe my grandfather's upbringing led him to understand and appreciate the meaning of life. He had a clear vision of living in harmony with God's plan and all the good things God wanted him to receive. God and faith in god are sources of inspiration that can coexist and my grandfather understood this. It was his continuous belief that through perseverance, determination, faith, setting a goal and seeing it through, God's healing power can transform us and ensure our achievement.

To Robert, success was not found in superficial material things, such as a showy car, expensive clothing, or extravagant trips, but in a life that expanded spiritually, socially and intellectually. As a young person, Robert made a spiritual commitment to his Christian faith, although he was tested time and again. The strength of his faith could not be overstated. It was repeatedly called upon when facing the many tragedies he experienced throughout his life.

Amid those tragedies, my grandfather had many positive experiences. His railroad journeys exposed Robert to many people from all walks of life. He even had the honor of escorting Henry Ford and Thomas Edison to their private car numerous times. My grandfather said Henry Ford's energy and mission focused on ensuring everyone in the United States was able to purchase a car and he respected that. One of the best days my grandfather remembered was escorting Thomas Edison to his private train car and sharing light hearted conversation with him. Mr. Edison expressed great excitement about Menlo Park being moved to Greenfield Village (now The Henry Ford). My grandfather said Mr. Edison was very approachable and he made a lasting impression on him when he thought about all his innovation. My grandfather had a sincere and deep appreciation of people and his natural ability to connect with them won him many friends. During his many travels, he reached out to people and encouraged them to walk with God and seek God's guidance on a daily basis. Robert made a deliberate effort to take time each day to meditate on God and specific Bible passages, such as one from the New Testament on steadfastness, *"Therefore, my beloved brethren, be steadfast, immovable, always abounding in the work of the Lord, knowing that your labor is not in vain in the Lord"* (1 Corinthians 15:58).

My grandfather told me that a year before his marriage and honeymoon, a terrible storm, known as the "White Hurricane," produced a blizzard with hurricane-force winds that brought terrible devastation to the Great Lakes from November 7 through November 10, 1913. On November 9, 1913, the storm was at its worst. In *Freshwater Fury,* Frank Barcus writes,

> *The storm on Lake Huron on November 9, 1913.—The storm of November 9 will be entered in the history of navigation as one of the most violent and one that exacted a greater toll of life and property on Lake Huron than any other storm within memory of local navigators… The survivors' accounts of the storm and of their struggle to keep their vessels afloat are almost heart-rending. The water, they claim, was simply a seething mass, such as they had never seen before. So helplessly were they tossed about by the waves and carried by the currents that most of them did not know where they were.*

A person has to wonder, with so much tragedy all around, where did the survivors find the strength to go on? Perhaps it is a testimony to the unseen, the power of faith and belief in a higher power that you cannot see or touch. Maybe it is a quiet confidence in God and having faith that no matter what is surrounding you, even though it may seem insurmountable, believing deep in your heart that you can rise above it, you will.

For over fifty years, my grandfather worked in every capacity for the railroad: laborer, locomotive driver, yard conductor, brakeman, switchman, and (near the end of his railroad days) passenger conductor. What was his attraction to the railroad? Was it the lure of faraway places and the beauty and design of the city and country landscapes? Or the healing power of the rhythm of the train, which has a life all its own as it seeps deep into one's thought processes? Perhaps it gave him calm and courage to accept the sorrow he faced and all of life's trials. Near the end of his time with the MCRR and later the New York Central line, he continued to work long hours six days a week. After fifty years of service to the Michigan Central Railroad, my grandfather retired in 1951 and received his gold pocket watch, the traditional send-off gift of appreciation to Railroad workers.

My grandfather possessed the gifts of compassion, engagement, perseverance and humor, and by using these gifts in his darkest hours, he was able to meet the challenges he faced. The self-discipline and determination he demonstrated on a daily basis, and the lessons in life he conveyed to me spoke to an undeterred inner strength and unwavering faith.

Chapter 2

STRUGGLES AND HEARTBREAK

"Why me?"

—*Ralph Kramden from The Honeymooners*

**GRANDFATHER, ROBERT JR. (BACKSEAT),
GRANDMOTHER (FRONT SEAT), circa 1935 (AUTHOR'S COLLECTION)**

My first memory of my grandmother is of her being fixed in a permanent rigid fetal position with hands and feet that were useless. The ever-present array of items, such as a wheelchair, folding dinner trays, special eating utensils, bedpans and diapers, became a significant part of my grandmother's life. It was physically difficult for Lillian to give grandmotherly attention and affection to me or my brother, Jim. However, my grandfather never failed to provide the much-needed attention and affection, all while maintaining his home, my parents' home and preparing meals.

As an adult, I learned that it was my grandfather who was the main caregiver, ensuring my grandmother was well cared for before he went off to work in the morning and then again in the evening. It was my grandfather who, after working a twelve-hour shift as a passenger conductor, would carry her immobilized body from a wheelchair to an armchair and then into bed, every day for the rest of her life.

My grandfather took over the management of the household when my grandmother's legs failed her. The serious side effects of the rheumatoid arthritis would eventually leave my grandmother totally dependent upon my grandfather and other caretakers. I watched in awe as my grandfather prepared meals, fed my grandmother, gently and lovingly looked after her daily living needs, washed the dishes, put the dishes away, and did the laundry. My grandfather ensured that everything was well maintained and through it all he never complained or seemed to have the time to think or relax. He just moved on to accomplish the next task at hand.

Lillian began to show the symptoms of rheumatoid arthritis in the early 1930s and was soon experiencing the slow deterioration of her overall functioning. My grandfather took care of my grandmother and over the next ten years, Lillian suffered major joint pain that made everyday tasks such as going up and down stairs, cooking, and housework impossible to complete. By age fifty, Lillian lost her ability to walk. As she continued to age, her weakened body revealed the ravages of rheumatoid arthritis in her arms, hands, feet, and legs.

Lillian was left at home most of the day, but luckily there were caring family members on a daily basis to provide assistance with her personal grooming, hygiene, and housework. Throughout the 1960s, Mary, my grandparent's African American housekeeper, provided additional help. I loved Mary as she was articulate, loving and compassionate. Mary was a significant part of our family and a trusted friend. Many years later, with tears in his eyes, my grandfather told me that our beloved Mary died. Mary had experienced a psychotic break with reality, was hospitalized and died in a state mental institution. I remember I cried and looked at my grandfather for an answer to my sadness and disbelief. He turned to me and said, "I know this hardly seems fair, but sometimes things happen in life that we have no control over."

Lillian was also a victim of the experimental "twilight sleep" anesthesia. This type of anesthesia was commonly used during the delivery of babies in the 1920s. My father, Robert Jr., was born November 28, 1923, at Henry Ford Hospital in Detroit. My grandfather believed the anesthesia caused my father's personality disorder, which included hoarding, a lack of social skills and a tendency to isolate himself, often with a spaced-out or faraway look in his eyes. This belief was not based on any research. I believe my grandfather had to construct a reason for my father's unusual personality. I believe it was difficult for my grandfather to accept the way my father was, and asked himself, "Why does he behave the way he does" on many occasions. My father had recurrent infections in his ears as a child and required adenoid surgery. After surgery, he lost the hearing in his left ear. Perhaps this was a part of his disconnect with others. He also suffered from chronic poor sleep and had difficulty learning new things.

My grandparents believed that it was possible to raise a "perfect" child based on the books and their teachings during this time. They were determined to raise a child with no imperfections or, as some would say, in a "normal state of rebellion."

This could have led to Lillian's over protectiveness and her codependent relationship with her son. My grandfather believed that the anesthesia used during the birth of my father was also responsible for the crippling rheumatoid arthritis my grandmother developed.

Wilbur Wright High School in Detroit was originally a school for the arts. It later became the city's leading vocational high school. My Father attended Wright and graduated in 1941. From conversations with my grandfather, I learned that my father had faced serious health problems during his youth. Due to the hearing loss in his left ear and his flat feet, he was not allowed into the military. In spite of these health problems, Robert Jr. did go on to find his first job driving a truck to deliver glass to businesses in Detroit. He later secured a second job as a hotdog vendor at Briggs Stadium in Detroit.

My grandparents did the best they could with my father. Unfortunately, he did not live up to their expectations that he would become a person who would instill greatness in others. Perhaps their expectations were unrealistic. He did prove to be a hardworking, dedicated man.

My Mother's Life before Hospitals

My mother, June Elizabeth Aldrich, was born June 19, 1920, in Niles, Michigan. Niles was settled in 1829, located where the Indian trails crossed the St. Joseph River. The first permanent settlers included the Walling, Lacey and Justice Families. They purchased the land from the United States government, platted and registered Niles in August, 1829, in honor of Hezekiah Niles. Hezekiah was a Quaker, and he published a highly regarded political newspaper that was distributed throughout the country.

My grandfather told me that thousands of slaves came through the Underground Railroad, particularly in the Niles area, and made their way through Michigan to freedom. Out of the seven different routes used to move escaped slaves through Michigan, Route 4 ran through the cities of: Niles, Vandalia, Schoolcraft, Kalamazoo, Battle Creek, Marshall, and Jackson. Route 4 became a major route to freedom from the South to the North.

From the *Fort Saint Joseph Museum, "Pasquel LaRue Finley, was born in Virginia in the early 1800's. He was very active in the Underground Railroad and transported fugitive slaves from Virginia to Kentucky and eventually into Ohio. He continued helping with the Underground Railroad when he moved to Niles in 1848.*

Because Michigan was close to Canada, a country that did not allow slavery, Michiganders played an important role in making the Underground Railroad successful."

There were thousands of slaves who risked everything to make their way through southern Michigan to newfound freedom in the North.

In the southwest corner of the state, near Marcellus, Michigan, there is a small cemetery situated near Finch Lake where Civil War veterans are interred. There lies my great-great-grandfather, Robert Lundy, who served as a soldier during the Civil War.

From Fort Saint Joseph Museum in Niles, *"Named for the brook that runs through it, Silverbrook Cemetery is older than the State of Michigan, having been founded in 1836 with lots sold to the public in 1838. Famous families buried in the Cemetery include the parents and sister of Montgomery Ward of catalogue fame; the family of Niles native journalist and sports writer, Ring Lardner; and the parents of John and Horace Dodge."* In addition, my ancestors on my maternal grandmother and maternal grandfather's side of the family are interred there. Civil War figures include Colonel Francis Quinn of the Michigan Twelfth and General Henry A. Morrow of the Twenty-Fourth Michigan Infantry.

From the Fort Saint Joseph Museum, *"The Four Flags Hotel, at the corner of 4ᵗʰ and Main Streets in Niles, was built in 1925 at a cost of $350,000 and was considered the most modern in Southwestern Michigan. It's reputed to have hosted Al Capone, Eleanor Roosevelt, Knut Rockne, and Truman Capote. It was the first business to adopt* *the name "Four Flags" and served as the cultural center of Niles for most of the 20ᵗʰ Century."*

There was a rumor that circulated on my mother's side of the family that my maternal grandmother and grandfather allowed Al Capone to store one of his getaway cars in their garage once.

According to the Fort Saint Joseph Museum, *"The Niles Rail Depot, a sandstone building, was completed in 1881. Its Neo-Romanesque style made it a real showplace, intended to impress visitors from the East with this last passenger stop before the Columbian Exposition in Chicago. Formal gardens were established in 1893 with a floating garden, a fish pond, a gazebo and a greenhouse that supplied flowers for the dining cars as well as for thousands of passengers who traveled through Niles, thus the affectionate title of "The Garden City." The depot has appeared in movies such as "The Continental Divide" with John Belushi, "Midnight Run" with Robert DeNiro, and "Only the Lonely" with Maureen O'Hara and John Candy."*

My mother was one of seven children who grew up in Niles during the worst period of the Great Depression era. As an adult, I learned that my mother's emotional needs had not been met during her childhood. Jule, my mother's younger sister, told me that my mother had temper tantrums from the age's three to six. Aunt Jule indicated my mother would hold her breath during the temper tantrum and go into a convulsion. My grandmother, Cora, helped my mother lie down and cushioned her head with a pillow and comforted her. Aunt Jule also stated that my mother fell down the basement stairs at the age of five and as a result had vision problems until, as an adult, she underwent surgery to correct her vision. I often wonder if this fall could have caused a head injury that triggered her mental illness.

For the most part, my mother had close relationships with her siblings, but a distant and unstable relationship with her own father. Having a large family to provide for and always struggling to find employment, my maternal grandfather, Edward Lorenzo Aldrich Sr., did not have much time to spend with my mother. My uncle Bob reported that after one night of drinking moonshine, my grandfather experienced temporary blindness. My mother's oldest brother, Edward, would receive a call almost every weekend from the local bar to come and pick up my grandfather and bring him home. It is no accident that my uncle Edward became a very responsible young man and adult.

My mother suffered from a lack of deep relationships and battled feelings of low self-worth. She wanted to have a deeper connection with her parents in which she could feel accepted for who she was and she wanted to have deeper communication with her siblings. My mother also desired to have an awareness of her own uniqueness and potential.

When I was a child, my mother told me her family had been very poor and that their desires as children for new clothes or birthday cakes went unfulfilled. Her parents struggled financially and had difficulty keeping up with the constant demands of providing for the seven children in the household. My mother recounted the time she invited twenty-five children from the neighborhood over to her house for her tenth birthday party. However, her parents did not plan any sort of party for her that day and she had to turn all the children away and return their gifts to them. All of this fueled her feelings of shame and disappointment.

After graduating from high school, each of my uncles enlisted in the military. They sought out the different branches of the military as a way to escape the poor conditions in which they grew up. They hoped enlisting would thrust them into creating their own individual achievements and they were right. Three of my uncles proudly served during World War II, in far-reaching places all over the world.

My uncle Ed enlisted with the army and served his country as a Sergeant for twenty years. While stationed in Germany during the war, my uncle Ed and my aunt Florence adopted a baby girl, my cousin Barbara, and brought her back to the United States to raise her. My uncle Richard served in the navy and was stationed in China, Japan and Okinawa. My uncle Richard was on an AKA- 60, an attack boat that was one of the first ships to arrive to Japan after the Japanese Instrument of Surrender was signed. My uncle Jim served in the army and was stationed in Belgium, France and the Philippians. Columnist Bill Moor from the South Bend Tribune writes, "He can still vividly recall his World War II days as a bridge carpenter attached to General George Patton's 3rd Army. After Jim helped finish a bridge over the Rhine River, he remembers Patton himself riding across it in his jeep while Jim and his engineering unit lined it. "I can still see him yelling out, "Good job, men." While building that bridge, Jim said shots were fired over it from both sides of the front. Some things, he wishes he couldn't remember. He ended up in Nuremberg, Germany, after falling 20 miles short of seeing Paris.

During his Army service, Jim also guarded invasion maps in a British warehouse during D-Day, patrolled a bridge across the Meuse River while the Germans tried to bomb it and was on a troop ship headed for the Philippines when the war ended. And then like most World War II veterans, Jim returned home, got married, raised a family and helped make the country go. He is a member of what we now fondly call the Greatest Generation."

My uncle Bob served his country during the late 1950s, as an engine mechanic in the air force, and was stationed in the lush Azores Islands. According to my uncle Bob, though the islands were very captivating, ultimately he just wanted to return home to Michigan.

Swept Away

My maternal grandfather's two brothers, Byron (Bunt) V. and James Aldrich, from Vandalia, Michigan, were originally blacksmiths during World War I. In 1926 they changed their profession. For the next twenty-three years they supplied various types of brooms for all of southwestern Michigan and northern Indiana. The broom corn came in bales from Illinois. Byron and James did all the actual work which included: separating the bales, tying it in bundles, dipping it in water that contained green crystals to give color, and then smoked it in an outside building for four hours. Then the corn was brought back into the shop. A handle was inserted in a clamp, a wire put through a small hole in one end, and corn was placed under the wire as the handle turned. The short corn was placed on the inside, and the longer fibers were placed on the outside.

BACK ROW, LEFT TO RIGHT: CORA (LUNDY) ALDRICH, EDWARD L. ALDRICH, JIM ALDRICH, BILL GLASBY, CECILIA, ERNIE (CECILIA'S SON), BRYON, MYRA, ADRIAN, PERRY, (MUSSIE IN FRONT OF PERRY), CECIL, AND UNCLE JIM'S WIFE, LENA

FRONT ROW, LEFT TO RIGHT: MARY (CECILIA'S DAUGHTER), JAMES, GREAT-GRANDMA ALDRICH (HOLDING MARY), ADRIAN'S SONS WOODROW AND OLLIE (SAILOR SUIT), GREAT-GRANDPA JAMES ALDRICH (HOLDING UNCLE ED), AUNT MYRA (HOLDING UNKNOWN CHILD). (AUTHOR'S COLLECTION)

I have fond memories of visits to uncle Byron and his wife, Myra's home in Vandalia, Michigan. Visiting there gave me a marvelous sense of freedom. We bounced along the bumpy roads that led to their home, and stopped along the way to picnic in Cass County. After the Civil War, during the 1880s, Vandalia was a stop on the Underground Railroad.

Aunt Myra had a large garden in the back of the house where she grew tomatoes, corn, beans, rhubarb and beets.

Nearly every time I visited I observed the huge front porch with yellow gladiolas and red hollyhocks growing all around it. When you walked into the house, the first thing you noticed was the massive mahogany staircase winding upstairs and the dark mahogany woodwork in every room. The dining room had a large oak table and twelve chairs for family dinners on Sunday or family reunions. There was always the smell of home cooking as you entered the home, such as freshly baked chocolate cake or strawberry-rhubarb pie. As we pulled up in front of the house, aunt Myra excitedly informed uncle Byron that we had arrived and enthusiastically led us into her home for an extraordinary weekend of great conversation, good food and laughter.

A New Beginning

My mother, June, attended Central High School in Niles and graduated in June, 1940. A few years after graduating from high school, my mother was offered the opportunity to move to Detroit to care for her ailing uncle Clyde, my maternal grandmother's brother, and his wife, Ann. My uncle Richard told a funny story about how in past visits to his childhood home in Niles, uncle Clyde and aunt Ann would sleep in my maternal grandparents' bedroom. After each visit, the mattress would have to be restructured due to the fact that uncle Clyde and aunt Ann were not small people.

After six months, my mother decided to stay in Detroit and located a job as a cashier at a local Kroger grocery store.

My parents met at Nardin Park Methodist Church in Detroit and dated for six months. My mother told me a story of when she first started going out with my father. Twice he arrived with a carload of women to pick her up for their date. After the two occurrences, my mother gave him an ultimatum, "Get rid of the women, or I will not be seeing you anymore." He eliminated the extra women in the car. In spite of the extra women, my mother fell in love with the man who listened to Swing Era records, dressed well, and was a "fun kind of a guy."

By the end of 1944, my parents were engaged and were married on February 14, 1945, in my father's childhood home on Dailey Avenue in Detroit. On their wedding day, my mother wore a dark brown suit with a corsage on her wrist, and my father wore a black suit with a red tie. Shortly after the marriage ceremony, the young couple honeymooned in Montreal. This puzzled my mother, as it was the middle of the winter, and the last place she wanted to be was shivering in a cabin in a remote part of Canada on her honeymoon. I believe it was a romantic gesture on my father's part. However, over time, my mother believed it was just the beginning of my father's odd behavior and strange occurrences that would become a significant part of my mother's life in the days ahead.

CHAPTER 3

EXTRAORDINARY COURAGE

One person can make a difference, and everyone should try.

—*John F. Kennedy*

During the 1950s on Dailey Avenue, my grandparents observed the direction and rapid change of their upper-middle-class neighborhood. Even before the Civil Rights Act of 1964, race was never an issue for my grandparents. For Robert and Lillian, many new neighbors also became trusted new friends for them.

In 1954, the minister of the Nardin Park Methodist Church began to express a need for an outreach program to include more African-Americans living in the neighborhood. My grandfather spoke out for the rights of his new African American neighbors, but sadly for him many of the parishioners ostracized him for voicing his approval on this idea.

On a clear September morning in 1954, my grandfather would soon discover the world around him changing dramatically. As my grandparents arrived at church and were seated in one of the dark mahogany pews, the choir sang the old hymn, *"What a Friend We Have in Jesus."*

During the sermon, the minister spoke about how, as Christians, the parishioners should reach out to the African Americans living in the surrounding community and endeavor to assist in any way they could. My grandfather bowed his head at the end of the sermon and thanked the Lord for all the blessings in his life. My grandfather also thanked the minister for his sermon and stated firmly and clearly that he agreed with all his positive affirmations regarding the need for inclusion to the African Americans now residing in the community. The sermon had a profound effect on my grandparents.

As they exited the church after the sermon, a sudden wind whipped up and blew my grandfather's brown fedora off. He ran after it and carefully placed it back on his head. While standing out in front of the church, many of the members shunned my grandparents for agreeing with the minister. My grandfather stood silently outside the church as the members avoided him. Robert held his head high, and with tears in his eyes, he proceeded to push my grandmother in her wheelchair toward their four-door 1950 black Ford sedan. It was the beginning of a painful time for them as they were no longer embraced by the parishioners they had known for so long. It did not seem to matter to many of the parishioners that the minister was espousing a belief that they needed to be reaching out to the African-Americans who were now a vital part of the community. It mattered deeply to my grandfather and the cynicism he encountered in the church was unacceptable to him. This had once been a place where he found solace and strength. Now it was just a lonesome place.

The Civil Rights Movement

The civil rights movement would change not only their lives, but also the lives of the people living around them. Sometimes, late in the evening, I heard my grandparents discussing the injustice of racism, the brutality of segregation, and how my grandfather desperately tried to change the views of many of the members of the Nardin Park Methodist Church, where they had once been members for over 30 years. Throughout the turmoil of the civil rights movement in the 1960s, my grandparents believed justice would prevail. Throughout my early childhood, I witnessed my grandparents' dedication to and respect for the numerous human struggles they were aware of within the African American community. I heard my grandfather speak about how African-Americans deserve the same opportunities to work and own a home as white people do.

Soon after their withdrawal from Nardin Park Methodist church, my grandparents decided to move and leave this neighborhood. Moving from this home on Dailey Avenue was one of my grandparents' most difficult decisions. My grandparents were one of the last original residents to move out of the neighborhood. Moving day arrived, and my grandparents sold their home on Dailey Avenue to another Williams' family who were African-American. They remained friends with them until my grandfather's death many years later.

**PATERNAL GRANDPARENTS' HOME ON DAILEY AVENUE, circa 1954
(AUTHOR'S COLLECTION)**

CYNTHIA (BABY), JIM (BROTHER), JUNE (MOTHER) AND ROBERT JR. (FATHER), circa 1953 (AUTHOR'S COLLECTION)

Looking back, after the Korean War ended in 1953, there was a surge in production for the automobile companies in Detroit, and with that, many people moved from the Appalachians to work in the automobile factories. Many African Americans moved to the north and Detroit during this time to escape from poverty and Jim Crow segregation and had aspirations of beginning a better life by working in the automobile plants in Detroit. For some, the opportunity to move into the working class did provide a better life. But for many of the African Americans now living in Detroit, it proved to be a negative reminder of the numerous social struggles they lived with in the South, such as segregated neighborhoods and schools, unemployment, and police brutality. Many years passed, and it would be 1961 before the civil rights movement made a strong social impact in Detroit when Martin Luther King spoke to a mass rally at Briggs Stadium.

I remember the summer of 1967, at age fourteen, when President Lyndon B. Johnson gave the order to send troops from the Eighty-Second Airborne from Vietnam into Detroit to stop the ensuing riots. I was informed by my grandfather that there was a curfew and all of the children in the neighborhood had to be in the house by seven o'clock in the evening.

My grandparents moved six miles away to a new neighborhood on Archdale Street in northwest Detroit. Throughout the turmoil of the 1960s and later the "white flight" of the 1970s and part of the 1980s, my grandfather remained in his "new" neighborhood as he approached ninety-four years of age. He was always friends with his neighbors, regardless of race. He reached out to the neighborhood children and taught each of them to play checkers, dominoes, chess, and to operate the Lionel train that was perpetually set up in the basement, just as he did so many times with me.

Nostalgic Memories

An early memory for me was going to picnics on Boblo Island with my grandfather. I was frightened the first time I rode on the Boblo boat on the Detroit River. I watched with great curiosity as the large, white boat sailed under the immense Ambassador Bridge. There was a live band playing Motown hits from the 1950s and 1960s and I danced along with other children on the boat until I was exhausted and fell down. Once on Boblo Island I rode the bumper cars, the Ferris wheel, the merry-go-round, rocket-to-the-moon (a strange rocket attached to a windmill type of building whose top would rotate), and took a train ride. There was always a picnic, with lots of grilled hamburgers and hotdogs. The adults and children would play amusing games, such as egg toss, three-legged races, and take part in pie-eating contests. I could really get worn out sinking my teeth into these activities.

Back at the house, my grandparents had a new twelve-inch, black-and-white TV in the living room. Most Sunday's I watched *Bill Kennedy's Showtime*, which was based in Canada from CKLW- TV in Windsor, Ontario.

One cold day in January in 1960, the Ambassador Bridge became the focal point of a funny story about Bill Kennedy, the Sunday movie time presenter. Alan Deneau, photojournalist for the *Detroit News*, was always on the lookout for a great story. Talk about being at the right place at the right time on a bitter cold day in January. Al had just arrived down at the old slaughterhouse located near the Ambassador Bridge on the Detroit side, and the story was that a bull had escaped and was making its way across the bridge to the Canadian side. The bull got to the Canadian side, and the Canadian police did not have guns at that time. The bull then turned around and headed back to the American side of the bridge. Suddenly, a twenty-year-old Rolls Royce pulled up on the American side on its way to Windsor. Out jumped Bill Kennedy, and with great flare, he threw his red scarf back over his shoulder and exclaimed, "Get that beast off the bridge! I have a show to do!" Shortly after this occurred, the bull came back to the American side of the bridge, and the American police shot the bull. They even cut its ear off just like they do in Spain during a bull run.

My grandfather, Robert, had a vast knowledge of history, partly from his years of study in becoming a 32nd degree Mason. He was a Mason for over sixty years, and at his death, he was the oldest thirty-second-degree Mason from the Detroit area. My grandfather was very familiar with the works of Charles Dickens, Jane Austen, F. Scott Fitzgerald, Mark Twain, William Shakespeare, Ernest Hemingway, and Abraham Lincoln and well into his old age, talked about these books and enlightened me as to the lessons they held. He frequently attended Masonic activities that included plays and concerts in Detroit. My grandfather told me about happy times he spent at Masonic Christmas parties from the early part of the twentieth century up until he was ninety-four years old. He remembered the thousands of bright, colorful balloons that were released from the ceiling to descend upon the children who were there every Christmas. Robert devoted many nights to the Shriners philanthropic events and the Shriners Hospitals for Children.

**VELMA, circa 1963 (MY FATHER'S COUSIN),
(AUTHOR'S COLLECTION)**

Time to Expand my Horizons

During the summer of 1963, my grandfather took me on a train trip to the Ozarks in Missouri. I remember a night train ride and an older gentleman sitting behind us, smoking a large smelly cigar. We had one stopover in Springfield, Illinois. It turned out we had to sleep in the train depot overnight to catch another train into St. Louis, where my father's first cousin, Velma, would pick us up. My grandfather was probably used to sleeping in strange places because of his days with the railroad. He placed a folded newspaper on top of his head and went to sleep. However, the depot presented challenges for me, as I sat on the hard, wood bench, swatting flies all night long. Once at my second-cousins home in the Ozarks, I relaxed and went swimming every day as the temperature soared well into the hundreds. On the last day, the trip was temporarily marred by a large green turtle biting me on my butt. I made a full recovery the next day, and just before we were to return home, I was able to see all the American Indian jewelry and handmade artwork at Velma's shop. The return trip was an overnight ride and we slept on upper berths in sleeper cars. I took in the excitement of the day and the long trip home in a warm July. The view from the window in my tiny room displayed the summer landscape with its green hues and deep blue sky, the wheat fields glowing in the afternoon sun, and the wheat stalks giving an impression of waving to you as you flew by. People seemed to magically disappear when the train made a stop. New people would appear, people with happy expressions, men wearing blue or beige summer suits, ladies with their little girls who wore braids, short bangs, and pretty summer dresses. I noticed a beautiful woman with dark hair wearing a small, black pill box hat with a veil attached covering her gray-blue eyes. My grand-father commented that the woman reminded him of Elizabeth Taylor, his favorite actress. We dined in the dinner car, and I was impressed by the porters who served us in their white waiter uniforms and white gloves. We arrived the next day in the early morning at Michigan Central Station in Detroit and took a cab home. Even then, my grandfather took precautions and pinned a container of money to his undershirt to avoid any pickpockets. I felt safe and grounded with my grandfather and could relish all the wonderful adventures and positive influences all around me.

Throughout his life, my grandfather did not indulge in extravagant trips, clothing, or automobiles. In order for him to meet expenses and to be generous, many times he took advantage of the inexpensive resources available to him. On one occasion, my grandfather took the entire family, for free, on the train to northern Michigan for the weekend.

According to my brother Jim, my grandfather took him under his wing at age eleven and helped him secure a paper route to give him something productive to do. Prior to this, Jim was quickly honing his skills as a petty thief. He was caught taking change from my mother's pocketbook on a weekly basis, so he could buy things that would keep him in the latest style of clothing. Because of my grandfather's persistence and guidance in turning my brother around, Jim continued to work as a paperboy for many years and befriended other boys, who have remained his friends throughout his life.

My grandfather also had great insight into many of life's challenges and temptations and was gracious enough to share that insight with my brother and me throughout our developmental years. When I was four years old, I became sick after eating too much Sanders vanilla ice cream. Later, my grandfather realized what I had done and he gave me my first taste of Vernor's Ginger Ale. Vernor's Ginger Ale was first introduced by a Detroit pharmacist, James A. Vernor, in 1866. There were other "elixirs" out at that time, including Coca-Cola, which contained alcohol. I remember when Vernor's was made on Woodward Avenue with the bearded troll on the bottle. It was love at first sip for me, and to this day whenever I am sick, Vernor's Ginger Ale is the only thing I want.

**LILLIAN (GRANDMOTHER), CYNTHIA AND JIM,
circa 1957 (AUTHOR'S COLLECTION)**

A Contrast in Temperament

Those easy times were something to hold on to when all was not so simple living with my mother. In the summer of 1957, when I was four years old, my mother informed us that she had planned an all-day outing on Belle Isle in Detroit. Belle Isle is larger than Central Park in New York City and in 1904 it held the nation's first freshwater aquarium along with the world's only marble lighthouse. Belle Isle was and remains a special place for families to visit year round.

My mother anticipated this would occur on a warm summer Saturday in June. However, on the morning of the outing, the weather appeared dark and cloudy, and the forecast called for rain. In spite of my father's protests, my mother was determined that we would go on a daytrip and have a picnic.

The 1949 black Ford my father owned was loaded up with food, pop, paper plates, napkins, cups, and blankets. My mother's happy mood quickly disappeared as we drove away from our house on St. Mary's Street because her foot went into the hole in the floor board. My father tried to cover the hole with a mat, but sometimes it did not seem to make a difference. Just as my mother started yelling at my father, "Bob, can't you fix this hole in the floor?" it started to rain. I looked at my brother and I took a deep sigh. My father tried as best he could to reason with my mother, "June we just don't have the money to fix it or to buy another car." If that wasn't enough, my father hit something in the road, and I heard the explosion of the rear tire as it went flat. My father pulled into the first gas station he saw, and the mechanic said he could put the spare tire on and that would have to suffice for the time being. All I could smell was gasoline as we waited for the mechanic to change the tire. I longed to just go home, and I breathed a sigh of relief as my father paid the mechanic and then declared, "We are going home now!"

Illuminating Memories

My brother, Jim, shared a story with me about an evening he had spent out with some friends at the age of thirteen. That evening he played spin the bottle and smoked his first cigarettes. After breaking many of the social rules of 1959, he settled in later that night to sleep in the next bedroom. My grandfather quietly, but pointedly, indicated he was concerned that my brother had stayed out too late. Then, without indicating that he may have smelled it, he told my brother how serious and hazardous smoking can be for young people his age and that he hoped he would never take it up. Naively, my brother wondered how he could have known. My brother was one of the few in his eighth grade circle who never took up smoking, despite great peer pressure at that time.

Loneliness

Early in 1959, my mother befriended an older gentleman, Ernie, to whom she shared her feelings of dissatisfaction about her marriage and her inability to find real happiness in her life. I saw that my mother seemed happier when she spent time with Ernie. My mother kept this relationship hidden from my father, and as far as I know, my father never found out about Ernie. I remember Ernie because he was very kind to me. One day, after a daytrip with Ernie, I heard my mother crying and talking to someone on the phone. Ernie had died that day from a massive heart attack. That was the last time I heard any more talk about Ernie. I think Ernie represented a father figure my mother desperately missed in her life. I liked Ernie and had mixed feelings about how I felt for my mother. I could see at times she was lonely, but felt sad for my father who was betrayed.

One wonders what was going through my mother's mind one amazingly sunny, spring day in 1959 when I was six years old, after Ernie had died. I remember seeing my mother in the front bedroom standing near the glass pane window. I saw tears running down her face, and suddenly she slammed her right hand into the window. I began to cry at the glass shattering and blood coming out of her hand and the next thing I remember was a neighbor, Mrs. Crammer, coming toward me, sweeping me up in her big, strong arms, and taking me to her house. As an adult, looking back at this incident, the whole thing seems inconceivable to me.

Helpless and Overwhelmed

Was she suicidal? Stricken with a dreaded disease? Or was this the beginning of a painful reality that she knew only as *major depression*? What in her life could have been so awful as to cause her to intentionally smash her hand into a glass windowpane? I witnessed this suffering not once but repeatedly over the next decade and with greater force, trauma, and sorrow. There were many days I would have walked ten miles or more, in the worst of weather, just to get away from her. I never ran away but did use my bicycle as a way to put plenty of space between us.

Shortly after the window smashing occurred, my father called my grandfather and told him he had better come over right away. It was late in the afternoon and Jim and I were instructed by my grandfather to walk to the back of our yard and stay near the red swing set until he came back to get us. Then he hurried back to the house. I did not know what was going on, but I had that instinctive feeling in my stomach that it was something bad. It all seemed like a dream. One look at my brother's devastated face, and I realized it was some serious unspoken thing having to do with my mother. I could hear faint crying, screaming, and the voice of a woman far off in the distance. My brother looked sadly at me and told me not to worry, that we would be going to grandpa's house. I did believe him and trusted him. He was seven years older than me. We were close by circumstances and sometimes by choice. But I felt sad, disappointed, and emotionally unsettled as I waited there. Unbeknownst to me, the first of what would be many in the years to come of my mother's psychotic breaks with reality had occurred that cool, spring day. Waiting there in the backyard, I remember feeling nauseated and time was slowing to a painful crawl. My grandfather was my anchor and I depended on him for everything. Little did I know or have an understanding at this young age of the numerous struggles and sacrifices my grandfather would make as he was put in a position to come to the aid of my parents over and over again.

Suddenly we were liberated from the yard, and my grandfather gestured for us to come with him. Our mother was gone. As Jim took my tiny hand and walked me to the front door of our house, I felt tears streaming down my face. I felt very sad and wondered when I would see my mother again.

Later that evening, as I sat at the bottom of the stairs, I overheard my grandfather talking on the phone to a close family member saying, "We almost lost her, Eileen." I would later learn my mother had physically assaulted my grandfather in his efforts to assist my mother to get ready to be transported to the hospital. She had had what was termed at that time "a nervous breakdown" and a break from reality.

The Battle with Depression

The "breakdown" meant that the person was unable to function in daily activities due to difficulties with adapting to the environment they were in. "Nervous breakdown" does not mean that nerves breakdown per se, but is used to describe an acute, time-limited phase of a specific disorder that presents primarily with features of anxiety and depression. According to the *Diagnostic and Statistical Manual of Mental Disorders, Fourth Edition (DSM-IV)*, it indicates that the nearest diagnostic category to nervous breakdown is adjustment disorder with mixed anxiety and depressed mood (acute). The nervous breakdown may have many features of mixed anxiety-depressive disorder, but the definition reveals a chronic condition, in contrast to the short-term nature of a nervous breakdown. The cause of major depression with psychotic features is not known. I now know that a family history can be a major contributor and bipolar disorder and depression run in my mother's family.

My mother required immediate hospital care, and the antipsychotic medications used today were not available back then. Instead electric shock treatment, which is known today as electroconvulsive therapy (ECT) was the prescribed treatment. It is the oldest, biological intervention in psychiatric antidepressant treatment for patients suffering from severe and medication-resistant major depression and mania. By 1930, ECT was used extensively along with surgery and medications. There were risks and side effects such as cognitive impairment, memory loss, and medical complications. In an article written by Lawrence Stevens, JD, he indicates, *"Defenders of ECT say that because of the addition of anesthesia to make the procedure painless, the horribleness of ECT is entirely a thing of the past. This argument misses the point. It is the mental disorientation, the memory loss, the lost mental ability, the realization after awaking from the 'therapy' that the essence of one's very being is being destroyed by the 'treatment' that induces the terror—not only or even primarily physical suffering."*

Over time, my mother's hospitalizations, which became an almost annual occurrence, would be longer and the continued use of ECT would take its toll on my mother's cognitive and physical state over and over again. It surely must have been extremely frightening for my mother to wake up after the treatments were over. It must have been like waking up from a horrible dream, wondering what happened during the time the person has no memory of.

I quickly learned that my grandfather, Robert, was committed to me through all of this tragedy. Just as importantly, my grandfather taught me that I was not powerless and that I could choose to move from victim to survivor. By learning to use tools such as my sense of humor, problem-solving abilities, my sense of purpose, my social competency, my autonomy, and my ability to thrive, I could get there. I personally witnessed my grandfather use these tools over and over again, particularly on a daily basis with my mother and this had a major impact on me.

What uncontrollable emotion overtook my mother in the fall of 1962? I had witnessed my mother display her anger and frustration toward my father many times. My mother had a lot of pent-up emotions and she vocalized her feelings of unhappiness and powerlessness in relation to her marriage. She told this to anyone who would listen. She was not a happy person and did not seem to possess the coping skills to handle the problems she had to face.

One day I happened to come home early from a friend's house. My only wishes that day were to ride my bike and feel the wind streaming through my hair. Letting my bike fall on the ground, I approached the front door to my house and witnessed my mother lashing out at my father in a fit of rage. I felt sad, embarrassed, and seriously concerned for my father. My father, although hardworking, still did not possess the strong sense of purpose, and determination that was ever present in my grandfather. My mother proved to be both verbally and physically assaultive toward my father and showed no remorse for her out-of-control behavior. Personally, I believe she did not think she had a purpose in life and all of her anger and frustration were a result of this thinking and were taken out on my father.

My mother had no boundaries at times, taking things out of my hands, throwing personal items away, and acting impulsively. When I was nine years old, Carol, my mentally challenged sister who was two years old, made it known to my mother that she wanted a doll that belonged to me. This doll happened to be my favorite doll. My mother, who was always easily irritated by my sister, told me to hand over the doll to my sister. Sadly, I complied, and this only added to the serious misgivings I felt about my mother. Looking back at my life at that point and not understanding the complexities of my mother's mental health issues, I could not comprehend why my mother would behave in such a cruel manner.

Luckily my grandparents' home was always open to me.

ROBERT AND LILLIAN WILLIAMS
GRANDPARENTS, circa 1959
(AUTHOR'S COLLECTION)

Appreciating the Simplicity of Everyday Life

I remember spending many days and nights at my grandparents' home on Archdale Street. The living room had a Duncan Phyfe cherry wood secretary desk in one corner filled with books by Charles Dickens, Abraham Lincoln, and Mark Twain. Two tall floor oak lamps stood at each end of the room and beautiful red oriental rugs could be found throughout the house. When I opened the glass door to the book shelf and reached for a book, a musty odor drifted out. In the summer I felt the cool, summer breeze that made the sheer, white curtains flutter gently coming in through the living room windows. When I opened the linen closet in the hallway, there were stacks of white, cotton sheets and pillowcases neatly folded, which had the scent of outdoors. One day I opened the linen closet door, and was stunned when a large stack of sheets and towels tumbled down on the top of my head. "Ouch!" My grandfather laughed when he arrived to help me pick them up.

I could hear the oscillating fan in another corner of the living room and smell tuna casserole baking in the oven. This was a favorite dish of my grandfather, probably because it was easy to make and relatively inexpensive. My grandfather was naturally thrifty and recognized the value in that.

Some days I saw the bookmobile making its rounds through the neighborhood as I rode my bicycle up and down the city blocks, waving to neighbors I knew. I recall the sounds of summer and listening to the crickets and katydid's at night, the hushed conversations between my grandparents, and Claude Debussy's "Clair de Lune" playing softly in the background.

I remember tuning in to WJR for my grandfather and listening to opening day at Briggs Stadium. The deep distinctive voice of Ernie Harwell would fill the afternoons and evenings, by giving the play-by-play of Tiger baseball. Harwell would lure me off to sleep most nights when I lived with my grandfather. He called the games at "The Corner" (Michigan and Trumbull Avenues) from 1954 on. It was evident, from the radio dial being set at WJR 760 throughout my childhood and all the games that my grandfather would talk about, that my grandfather loved Tiger baseball as much as Ernie Harwell did.

OPENING DAY 1960 AND THE DETROIT TIGERS RUNNING OUT OF THE DUGOUT AT BRIGGS STADIUM, LATER TO BE NAMED TIGER STADIUM (PHOTO COURTESY OF ALAN DENEAU)

Harwell, *The Corner,* pages 17 and 218-219

We're all going to miss Tiger Stadium, but we just have to keep the old ballpark in our minds and our souls and look at it that way rather than as a building that's been knocked down. But there are a lot of memories. Opening Days, for one thing, have always been special. And it was an Opening Day when Kirk Gibson got hit in the head by a fly ball when he was playing right field. One of the worst things that happened was around 1972. We had a Friday night game with the California Angels, and it was raining. We got a phone call from Hal Middlesworth, the publicity director, and he said, "If the game's called, we'll have a doubleheader Saturday. But don't announce it until you hear from me." So Stits (engineer Howard Stitzel) and Ray Lane and I were in the booth when we heard this voice on the intercom: "Game postponed; doubleheader Saturday." So I put it on the air. My wife, Lulu, came to the game and we were going to hear a friend sing in Plymouth. As we were going out of the ballpark, I noticed a lot of people weren't leaving. I figured that was kind of strange but thought they just didn't want to get wet. So we went out and got on the expressway and tuned into Ray Lane doing the postgame show, giving the scores. All of a sudden he said, "Wait a minute, folks, that announcement Ernie made wasn't right. The game is still on. Ernie! Ernie! Wherever you are, come on back." "So I turned around and came back to the booth and we did the game."

Peaceful Times

In June 1961, when I was visiting with my grandparents, I remember traveling along with them in their light blue 1960 American Motors Rambler. We would go to Lansing for weekend visits to one of my father's cousin's farms. I would sit in the backseat and my eyes would barely be visible peeking out of the rear side window. As I glanced out the window, I noticed the colors of summer, the viridian green grass, the cerulean blue sky, and a green passenger train going by as we waited patiently at the gate in Plymouth and then on for a brief stop in Ann Arbor.

Once we stopped in Ann Arbor to visit my aunt Ruth, and I heard my grandparents say, "Poor thing. Ruth will always be an old maid" and "Ruth is a human wreck." My middle name comes from my father's aunt Ruth and I silently wondered to myself, is that my destiny? Once back in the car, I felt safe, content, and happy-go-lucky. I was at peace for the time being and happy wearing the new white headband that pulled my dark auburn hair back, blue shorts, a white sleeveless cotton top, white bobby socks and white Keds sneakers that my grandfather had bought for me the day before our trip. I was a tomboy and wanted nothing to do with cute little, pink, lacy dresses and black, patent leather shoes. I enjoyed a good game of baseball in the middle of the street or field or the playground in the back of Coolidge School. I believed I could compete with any of the boys.

After visiting aunt Ruth, I was thrilled to have finally arrived in Lansing at the farm. The farm belonged to my father's cousin, Harley, and his wife, Ethel. Harley had three children and one of his daughters, Charlotte, was my age. We had fun playing hide-and-seek in the barn. We rode our bikes down the road to the old-fashioned country store, with faded white paint on the outside and the American flag hanging prominently near the door. An older woman, with her hair swept up in a bun and wearing a cotton housedress with little red flowers on it, sat on the porch. Next to her was a box, which was full of kittens. With a twinkle in her eyes, she asked us, "Do you want to adopt one of the kittens?" Charlotte politely turned her down and we entered the store to purchase a pound of butter for dinner that evening. We all sat down to supper in the large dining room, with a white linen table cloth covering the walnut table, white china, and tall glasses of lemonade, and enjoyed corn on the cob and fresh ripe tomatoes from the garden.

I quickly became friends with the horses, cows, chickens, ducks, and wild kittens running around outside and grew to appreciate their simple beauty. The smell of fresh hay, newly cut grass and lilacs hung in the hot, humid air late into the day. Weeping willow trees could be seen near the front of the freshly painted farm house. The large green trees moved to the wind, and I lay under one of them for hours, aware of their motion, daydreaming about living on the farm as the trees transported me to a peaceful place.

Down the dusty country road a bit was a reminder of a baseball diamond, complete with old bleachers, the paint worn white by years and years of sun and rain. Harley said I could play with an old bat, baseball, and a glove. I threw the ball up and then hit it as hard as I could. It was evident that no one played there anymore, but I used my imagination and pictured I was a star hitter for my team. I ran around the imaginary bases to home. Only it wasn't home. It was a temporary diversion from my real life. My beautiful summer weekend was short-lived, and the country sights and sounds slowly began to fade from my eyes and ears. It took all my courage and strength to prepare myself mentally for the return home to my mother.

Hospitalization Looming on the Horizon

When I was eight years old, my mother was hospitalized again, and I went to stay with my grandparents. I remember my grandmother, impressing me with her sharp mind and keen wit, despite appearing to be fatigued or in great pain. It was a humbling experience to be in my grandparents' presence. In 1962, when I was nine years old, I spent most of the spring and half the summer with my grandparents. On a bright, beautiful day in late May, my mother was taken away on a gurney into the white ambulance to Wyandotte General Hospital with the sirens blasting. I was at school this time and as I was walking down my street I saw the ambulance speed away. Hurt and scared I came home and found out that my mother had had a psychotic break with reality again. My grandfather was there and held me tightly as I sobbed. My grandfather said, "Now, now, chin up. Be a good soldier, Pack up your things and let's go." I stepped into my grandfather's car and into the familiar safe and loving surroundings I had come to rely upon.

When school ended for the summer, I dreamily lay on my twin bed upstairs, with a white chenille bedspread and feather pillow covered by a white linen pillow case. I read poems from Emily Dickenson and books by Mark Twain such as *Puddn'head Wilson*, *Adventures of Huckleberry Finn*, *The Adventures of Tom Sawyer*, *Literary Essays*, *Sketches New and Old*, and *The $30,000 Bequest and Other Stories*. My father did have a strong work ethic and he secured a job working as a laborer for the New York Central Railroad. My brother was off with his many friends, and on my own, I was able to push past my grief over my mother leaving me again. With the help of these books and stories, my spirits were lifted.

Most days, I would lie outside in the backyard under a large, old oak tree and feel the intense heat of the sun and a faint breeze on my skin as I ate wild raspberries I had picked there the day before. Late in the summer, for many years, my grandfather would let me pick raspberries that grew in the far end of the backyard. Many times I wished I could remain lost back there, hidden in the raspberries, where it was peaceful. I was carefree for a while. Once I was in the raspberry patch at my grandfather's house, I felt safe. I drew seascapes and lighthouses in summer colors, with the sunset fading into the background.

As I grew older, I learned to develop and hone my skills as a painter and developed a strong passion for oil painting and art. It became more than a way to pass time. I believe it saved me in many ways because it became a strong, positive force in my life and helped me discover a tranquility within myself which was later reflected in my artwork.

One night, as I closed my eyes and started to fall asleep upstairs at my grandfather's house, off in the distance I heard a train whistle as it rolled through the summer evening on its way across the Midwest, and it became very clear to me that my siblings and I were emancipated for now.

Wading through Sorrow

Hospitals became a constant part of my early life during the 1960s. Once, in early 1961 when I was eight years old;

my father was admitted for a month to a psychiatric unit at Northville State Hospital and diagnosed with schizophrenia. I do not believe this diagnosis was accurate, as many patients back in the early 1960s were diagnosed with schizophrenia. It was evident that his peculiarities had become more pronounced after a period of marriage and especially when dealing with the demands of raising children.

**NORTHVILLE STATE HOSPITAL, JULY 2012
(PHOTO COURTESY OF STACEY REYNOLDS)**

There were many times in my youth when I tried to convince myself that my father was like everyone else's father, but deep down, I knew he was not. Once when I was a child, I told my friends, "He is not my real father." It hurt too much to tell the truth, so I would not admit he belonged to me. I did not have any illusions about my father. From an emotional standpoint, I tried to maintain at a distance and just hold onto all the bright possibilities that life held for me. As my father got older, he often appeared to be in his own world. He would not socialize, acknowledge or talk to me. My father was troubled over his adult responsibilities and simply could not function. From my observations, my father appeared to function in a disconnected way.

In late August 1962, I went on a daytrip with my grandparents to visit relatives who lived in Ann Arbor. As we traveled to Ann Arbor, not wearing seatbelts as was the custom in those days, we were in an accident. A vehicle swerved right in front of us, and we collided. My grandmother sustained injuries from being thrown against the dashboard, which caused internal bleeding, infection, and gangrene in her legs. Once my grandparents returned home, my grandmother's two sisters, Lottie and Eleanor, immediately got involved with my grandmother's care. The sisters insisted that my grandmother have her legs amputated at the University of Michigan Hospital in Ann Arbor.

Unbeknownst to the sisters, Lillian privately had indicated to Robert and her doctor that there would not be any further treatment or surgery. Sadly for my grandfather, like so many other difficulties and tragedies he faced, Lillian's refusal to follow up with treatment at the University of Michigan Hospital, led to the end of his relationship with the two sisters. This was particularly heart wrenching for my grandfather, considering Lottie had suffered from alcoholism most of her life. I was a witness to my grandparents rescuing Lottie financially many times over the years. Lottie made it clear to my grandparents that she was disappointed with their decision and withdrew all physical and emotional support. My grandmother passed away at home not long after the accident.

Perpetual Light

In the winter of 1962, when I was nine years old, I became extremely ill with whooping cough. Despite strong advice and direction from my grandfather, my parents basically took no action in getting me the medical help I needed. All I remember is coughing and trying to get my breath. My grandfather stepped in and took me to the family physician, Dr. Husband. I thought I was going to die due to the relentless coughing. Thanks to my grandfather's love and Dr. Husband's persistence, I was able to recuperate quickly. Later I learned that a child can cough so hard that it could cause a hemorrhage and the child could die.

My mother's depression required yearly hospitalization from the time I was three until I was fourteen. Her hospitalizations caused abandonment issues in me. However, with my grandfather's love and guidance, he would reassure me that I was not carrying the burden of living with a mentally ill mother alone. Sometimes he would talk about everyday things, and other times he would be silent. He was always optimistic and would encourage me to focus on adjusting my attitude and learning something new every day. I could trust that my grandfather would be there for me if I needed to talk or cry.

I was reluctant to visit my mother at the hospital since it meant waiting alone, for what seemed like an eternity, in the waiting room. I was not allowed to visit my mother when we first arrived at the hospital. First my grandfather, father, and brother would visit my mother for a while, and then we would all be ushered into a room to visit together as a family for a short time. The time flew by as my mother sat in a high-back, red leather chair and barely spoke to me. Many times as a child, I felt as if I were watching myself in a movie, like the old 35 mm. reel-to-reel type, that seemed to be stuck and repeated the same scene over and over as I sat there weeping silently. The scene was watching my mother beginning to behave in a broken way, alienated from me, spiraling downward, becoming more and more depressed and isolated. I watched helplessly as she lost touch with reality. I worked hard to block it all out, but the terrible images of my mother turning into a person I did not recognize would not withdraw from my mind or my heart. As I sat there, I nervously played with a string of pearls I wore around my neck, twisting and twirling them around. My grandmother Williams had given me this necklace before she died. I wished I were on a long train adventure, traveling across the country, watching the sun set on the ever-changing terrain and seeing myself in completely different circumstances.

Later in the evening, after we returned from visiting my mother, I overheard my grandfather talking to a relative on the phone. I learned my mother had just endured psychiatric shock treatment for the major depression she was experiencing. The shock treatment was considered successful because within four weeks the symptoms of depression disappeared. As a child I did not fully understand what that meant. We would, once again at my grandfather's home, return to our routines.

Each visit to the psychiatric floor at Wyandotte General hospital to see my mother would stir up an unsettling wave of fear that would pass over me and remain for a long time. It was with great reluctance and guilt that I would return to my mother's care once she was discharged. Perplexed, I wondered how long before my world would spin out of control again.

**A GLIMPSE OF OUR HOUSE ON ST. MARY'S IN DETROIT, 1950
(AUTHOR'S COLLECTION)**

The Contrast between Two Homes

After my mother was discharged from the hospital, my father, mother, brother, sister, and I returned to our house on St. Mary's Street. I later observed the heart-wrenching consequences of the electroconvulsive shock treatment my mother had to endure. I witnessed the forgetfulness, the lack of emotion, and an almost fogginess that followed for two months after she came home. How could anything go back to the way it was before my mother's hospitalizations?

The house on St. Mary's Street was a modest house with no basement and very few comforts. Cold in the winter and rather run down, it had wood floors, a stove with a large pipe going into the wall in the living room to provide heat, two small bedrooms, and a small bathtub with claw feet, an attic that was difficult to get into, a small garage, and a porch with a white railing.

The small kitchen had a refrigerator crammed in a corner near the backdoor, and occasionally mice would show up when my mother would be cooking dinner. We knew when the mice appeared because my mother could be heard screaming and scrambling to get to higher ground on a red vinyl chair. Many dinners that my mother cooked were not particularly appetizing. Forget about fresh vegetables; everything was boiled beyond recognition. I always found clever ways to avoid them, and I became very adept at deliberately tossing food behind the refrigerator. At my grandparents' home, it was a different story. My grandparents had a beagle named Skipper. I threw food I did not want under the table, and the dog would gobble it up, thereby erasing the evidence.

When I was six years old, I went to Mt. Carmel Mercy Hospital to have my tonsils removed. I was there longer than usual because I had a cold and Dr. Husband had to wait until I recovered from it before he could perform the surgery. I liked Dr. Husband because he looked a lot like Myron Floren, the accordionist on the Lawrence Welk Show. Night after night, no one came to visit me. I was sad about this at first, but on the third night, I wondered, what is this all about? On that particular night, the last group of nurses checked on all of us in the large ward. I grew bored and decided it was time to shake it up in that room. I went around to each child's bed and cranked the bed up and down with the lever. "Look," I said, "the nurses and the nuns have gone to bed! So let's have some fun!" Ginger ale went flying, and just as I was becoming an expert at bed cranking, the head nurse walked in the ward and screamed, "All of you children get into your bed and lie down immediately, or there will be consequences!" We all quieted down, and the next day I had my tonsils out. My parents visited that night and told me all about how they tried to visit the previous night but the car had broken down. I was just happy to see them. Upon returning home, I enjoyed lots of Sanders ice cream and pudding as I sat on our front porch on St. Mary's Street and recuperated.

By the time I was eight, the house on St. Mary's Street had been remodeled with white aluminum siding, an additional bedroom and utility room, a space heating system, and a new front porch. All the updates were done by the Italian next door neighbor's brother, Antonio. I remember the workers singing American Italian songs, such as "Fly Me to the Moon," by Frank Sinatra and "Rags to Riches," by Tony Bennett while they labored all day long, transforming our house into something aesthetically pleasing.

In contrast, at my grandparents' home everything was clean, orderly, and uncomplicated. I slept in the cozy upstairs and all my things were unpacked and placed neatly in drawers and the closet. When I awoke in the early morning, I heard the downstairs door creak open and the booming, reassuring voice of my grandfather, the passenger conductor, and call out, "All aboard!"—in other words, "Get up now!" If for some reason I did not respond to the call and get up, a cold washcloth would sail across the room and smack me in the face. This must have been an old railroad man technique to wake napping railroad men after taking too long of a lunch break. I can hear him asking his employee, "Did you forget about our Port Huron destination? You are delaying our departure! Now get up!" Breakfast would follow and would include one-inch-thick pancakes with lots of maple syrup. My brother and I would head off to school, and my father, who worked as a laborer, would head off to work at the Livernois railroad yard in Detroit. My sister, Carol, would remain at home with my grandfather during the daytime.

Living at my grandparents' home, I was often challenged to a game of checkers or chess. My grandfather got a lot of satisfaction from playing checkers and dominoes with me, and for some strange reason, I always won. As a child, I thought, "He isn't very good at these games." I later realized that he threw the games so my self-esteem could develop and grow. He continued this tradition with the neighborhood children long after I moved away.

CHAPTER 4

APPLE OF HIS EYE

I was to be the comforter of others even in my own distress.

—Jane Austen

The Detroit neighborhood that I grew up in during the 1950s and 1960s was idyllic. There was order in my surrounding environment that could be counted on to continue as time went by. Detroit was an exciting place to live and grow up in, a place to be thankful for, and that was irreplaceable. There were certain things I could count on, such as the little Italian bakery at the corner of Plymouth Road and Mettetal Street. I could see all around me the strikingly blue sky and the giant elm trees with their greenery as I navigated my bike through the neighborhood in the summertime. You could smell the fresh-baked goods and garlic two blocks away. The bakery was also my main source for my favorite red licorice candy. I remember riding my bicycle throughout the neighborhood all spring, summer, and fall, dropping it on the ground just outside the front door of my home and never giving a second thought as to whether it would be there the next time I came outside.

CYNTHIA WILLIAMS, circa 1955, ON ST. MARY'S STREET (AUTHOR'S COLLECTION)

The streets were lined with tall, beautiful elm, oak, and pine trees, flowers of every type, rockwork, and luscious lawns. Many of the homes had gardens that came back each spring lovelier than the year before. The neighbors to the left of my parents' home were transplanted from Italy and to look over the fence into their backyard was like catching a glimpse of Tuscany. Every day I would walk to our backyard to view the beauty of roses of every imaginable color and size that grew in their backyard and all along the steel fence between our houses. Mr. Asquini must have been heavily influenced by the Renaissance gardens from Florence because his garden had boxed hedges and statuary along with hundreds of brightly colored flowers. He had dark purple grapes growing on vines over an archway in their driveway.

The neighbors to the right were of Polish descent and were a mystery to me. Occasionally I did see their son Leonard walking nervously out the front door after being yelled at by his loudmouthed mother. When I was seven years old, Leonard gestured for me to come over to his backyard. It seemed Leonard wanted me to see the new fort he had built in the backyard. Shortly after I entered the fort, Leonard proceeded to try to convince me to play doctor with him. None of his efforts were successful and I ran home crying to my mother. When my mother confronted Leonard over the backyard fence about what had happened, he just shrugged it off without any sense of shame. My mother was visibly upset after she returned from the neighbors' house to report the incident to his mother. The neighbor had slammed the door in my mother's face, which sent my mother into a tailspin whereby she ranted and raved for hours about the incident and how the neighbors hated her. Due to her insecurity and low self-esteem, this proved to be just one of the many disconnects my mother would have with the neighbors, to which I would grow accustomed as a child.

From time to time, I noticed two of the neighbor ladies across the street from our house standing around pointing their fingers at my mother and gossiping about her as they stood on their front porches. I avoided them. But Mrs. Crammer, another neighbor farther down the street, was very accepting of my mother and just about every day would come by to check on my mother and me. I had terrible nosebleeds as a child and when my mother would fall apart over it, Mrs. Crammer in her charming, calm and lovable way would know exactly what to do to make them stop.

I remember as a little girl, Jim would flood the backyard in the winter and play hockey with his buddies from the neighborhood. He made an interesting discovery in his bedroom closet one day after he came home from school. To my embarrassment, he noticed I had moved some of his hockey equipment around and yelled, "Stay out of my room!" as I leisurely walked away from him. Who knows, but maybe he had plans to become the next Gordie Howe?

When Jim was eleven years old, he was instructed by one of his buddies on the other side of Plymouth Road to cross on his bike. Jim looked both ways and proceeded across the typically busy street. As the rapidly approaching bright red 1957 Chevrolet car hit my brother, he was thrown in the air, sustained a fractured skull, a minor concussion, and a broken leg. Mrs. Crammer came to the rescue again and consoled my panic-stricken mother and took care of me until my grandfather arrived to take over. My mother just did not seem to know what to do. It was the beginning of summer, and for the remainder of the summer, Jim sat on our front porch, bemoaning his misfortune. Riding his bike and social-izing with his friends on his paper route would have to wait while he mended.

CYNTHIA (BABY), JIM (BROTHER), circa 1953
(AUTHOR'S COLLECTION)

Between the ages of seven and fourteen, I rode my twenty-inch, blue Schwinn Hollywood starlet sting ray bicycle up and down the city streets most spring and summer days. I felt on top of the world. My grandfather had taught me how to ride the bike, which he had bought for me. How could I know at the time that this bike would be one of the greatest gifts my grandfather could have given me? It presented me with an opportunity to become more independent and to escape my mother's increasingly unpredictable, angry outbursts.

In the early 1960s, neighbors could be trusted to look out for each other and each family's children. If you were up to no good, the neighbors generally knew about it and would be compelled to provide a verbal account of your bad deeds to your parents or grandparents or both.

As I proceeded through the neighborhood on my bike, I would ride slowly past many of the homes and try to get a glimpse of what life must be like in other people's houses. Strange as it seems now, I hoped sometimes that I would get invited to a neighbor's barbecue or birthday party so I could be a part of a "normal family." I often wondered if birthdays were always so delightful for the neighbor children, with the parents running around ensuring that everyone was having a great time. I thought if I hung around awhile, through mental telepathy the neighbors would get this sudden urge to invite me to their holiday gatherings. I don't remember my birthday being acknowledged every year, or if it was, it was not with much fanfare.

**THE CELEBRATION ON WOODWARD AVENUE FOR FLAG DAY AND THE LARG-
EST AMERICAN FLAG UNFURLED OUTSIDE OF THE J.L. HUDSON DEPARTMENT
STORE, 1960 (PHOTO COURTESY OF ALAN DENEAU)**

I looked forward to Flag Day in Detroit, which involved members of the armed services and the general public as the Detroit Police Band played and marched down Woodward Avenue. The largest American flag could be seen outside of the third and ninth floors of the J.L. Hudson Department Store.

Families celebrated the Fourth of July by proudly displaying their American flags and by throwing parties with red, white, and blue streamers, paper plates, cups, and fireworks. During the 1960s, many of my neighbors made an annual trip to Ohio or Indiana to pick up fireworks because they were illegal in Michigan. They would stash them away until ready to start the show. It was a magical time. I knew that at around nine o'clock on the Fourth of July, the silence on the street would be broken by the mysterious sounds of firecrackers and bottle rockets. I sat on the front porch and gazed at the fireworks in the sky. As the night went on, I just believed this was the way everyone lived, and they were happy.

My best friend, Linda, lived one street away on Mansfield Street. I still remember the beautiful gardens and winding paths in her backyard. The sun would fall gently through the oak trees and onto a mass of wandering ivy that seemed to cover half of the backyard. Lilies-of-the-valley, red tulips, and pink peonies gleamed in the morning sunlight. As young girls, we would play hopscotch on the sidewalk and play in the backyard in the summer, creating tents and putting on little plays. One day, as I was playing hide-and-seek with Linda, the neighbor girl, Peggy, came over to join us. We rested for a while on the grass, and Linda's mom brought us Hostess cupcakes and a banana flip. Peggy was jealous of me because Linda was paying more attention to me than to her. The next thing I knew, Peggy took the banana flip and pushed it into my face. As I became very upset, with tears running down my face, Linda's mom came outside to clean me up. I did not run home because I knew it would upset my mother and she would become very angry about the whole situation. After being comforted by Linda's mother, who responded to me with compassion, I continued to play with Linda, and we created a lemonade stand whereby we enjoyed the remainder of that hot, summer day.

Sharing our Dreams

Other memories include times spent with my girlfriends at their homes, enjoying a pajama party. One particular night, about ten of us decided to run down the street to the corner drug store for some chips. This would not have aroused any attention if we had been dressed in our regular street clothes, but we all had our pajamas, slippers, and robes on and were challenging each other to race back to the house where the party was being held. At one point the girl in front of me suddenly stopped and turned around and with that I crashed into her. Consequently, a couple other girls crashed into one another, and we all lay on the ground in a big heap, laughing hysterically. The party night continued back at my friend's house, upstairs, with everyone participating in a séance to try to communicate with President John F. Kennedy, but nothing moved and no spirit talked to us. We asked childlike questions and turned the magic eight ball for the answers. The last event of the evening involved one of the girls at the party confiscating another's bra, wetting it, and putting it in the freezer. I enjoyed being accepted and part of the group. The next day I returned to the quietness and safety of my grandfather's home and went back to playing checkers with my grandfather.

The Book-Cadillac Hotel

My grandfather, Robert, attended many philanthropic events at the Book-Cadillac Hotel during its heyday. My grandfather deeply respected JFK, and just like JFK, my grandfather had a lot to cope with. However, he continued to persevere and have a passion for life. I believe he truly understood how much a child needs and longs for a parent's time and attention and is deserving of both. He always made time to encourage me to read or engage me in a game or a fun activity. He would also diligently share stories from what he had read in newspapers or books and personal stories from his childhood. When I was with my grandfather I felt safe. Thanks to his determination I could direct my attention to just being a child for a while and focus on having fun.

Mark Schmidt purchased a rocking chair for President Kennedy for his upcoming stay in the Presidential Suite. That same year, President John F. Kennedy visited Detroit to attend the Veterans Convention. This was the last time he was to visit Detroit.

PRESIDENT JOHN F. KENNEDY SHOWN HERE WITH MARK SCHMIDT,
MANAGER OF THE BOOK-CADILLAC HOTEL 1960
(PHOTO COURTESY OF ALAN DENEAU)

Olympia Stadium

From Kincaide's, *The Gods of Olympia Stadium: Legends of the Detroit Red Wings,* 131, *Gordie Howe,* "When I first came up to Detroit in 1946, I was worried about whether I could make it or not, yes. I felt that way for a while and then I ended up scoring 35 goals in 1950, my fourth season in the NHL. Then I wasn't worried anymore."

THE RED WINGS AT OLYMPIA STADIUM, 1954-55, THIRD GAME, 2ND PERIOD FOR THE STANLEY CUP, TERRY SAWCHUK, GOALIE, ALEX DELVECCHIO, PLAYER, LEONARD "RED" KELLY, PLAYER. JEAN BELIVEAU, HALL OF FAME AND LONG-TIME MONTREAL CANADIEN PLAYER WITH SCORING PLAY AND BOOM BOOM GEOFFRION, MONTREAL CANADIEN PLAYER KNOWN FOR HIS SLAPSHOT, BEHIND THE NET (PHOTO COURTESY OF ALAN DENEAU)

This was the third game of the Stanley Cup finals. Detroit lost this game but came back to beat Montreal in the best of seven series. After the game ended, there was a huge banquet held at the Book-Cadillac Hotel and everyone drank champagne out of the Stanley Cup. What was interesting was Maurice "Rocket" Richard, with the Montreal Canadiens, came to the ballroom and shook hands with Gordie Howe. The "Rocket" could go to any restaurant or bar and never had to pay. "Rocket" was like a hockey God. His brother was known as "Pocket Rocket" and he had a hard slap shot just like his brother.

**THE BEATLES PERFORMING AT OLYMPIA STADIUM, SEPTEMBER 6, 1964
(PHOTO COURTESY OF ALAN DENEAU)**

During the Beatles concert, photojournalist Alan Deneau was bombarded by jelly beans. Apparently Paul McCartney liked them and mentioned this in an interview prior to the concert. Screaming fans completely drowned out the Beatles music. Trying to park was difficult and entering the building was next to impossible. The press slipped in a back entrance to witness the pandemonium of 20,000 fans. Every once in a while a teenage girl would try to crash the stage. The police stepped in and carried them off. Amid a barrage of jelly beans and women's panties, photographer Alan Deneau still managed to capture some great shots of the "Fab Four."

The music scene was booming during the 1960s in Detroit. A historical musical event was taking place at the Olympia Stadium when the Beatles performed in downtown Detroit. I remember playing records on the record player, dancing in my bedroom, on the front lawn, and in backyard all summer long to the Beatles songs and Motown Record hits. My friends and I were dazzled by songs such as, "I Want to Hold your Hand" and "She Loves You" by the Beatles and "How Sweet it is To Be Loved By You" and "Ain't that Peculiar" by Marvin Gaye. By now, most Detroit radio stations were playing Motown Records hits, such as "Dancing in the Street" by Martha and the Vandellas and "Where Did Our Love Go" by the Supremes.

Hidden Treasures

My father, Robert Jr., was as a hoarder. He would always be on the lookout for "collectibles," such as the internal parts of a piano, stacks of newspapers, old crates, broken furniture, and other useless items. They would usually end up in the garage. I say "usually" because sometimes my mother would prevent my father from adding more junk to his collection. There must have been a powerful force driving him to continue his obsession year round. As an adult, I now understand that his hoarding behavior was one symptom of what would have today been diagnosed as obsessive-compulsive disorder (OCD). He was unable to discard useless items and created stacks of old pieces of paper in the bedroom and in the garage. My mother insisted that the garage door be closed at all times so the neighbors would not find out about his weaknesses and her growing anger and frustration surrounding it all. Another symptom of the OCD was his inability to make decisions and to isolate himself in social situations.

I lived in two worlds, a stable one with my grandfather and the unstable one with my mother. Velma, my father's cousin, stated that my grandfather, Robert Sr., thought of me as the "apple of his eye." I had a strong sense of this, but it was not until I was an adult that this sentiment was confirmed through a telephone conversation with Velma. The other world revolved around my mother, June, and her increasingly long periods of depression.

My grandparents lived one mile away from my parents' home, and their home was larger and more attractive than mine. After some remodeling during the late 1950s, the exterior had clean white siding with black trim, a large window in the front of the house, and aluminum awnings on the windows, a large garage, and a screened-in front porch, a long backyard with a pen for my grandparent's dog, Skipper, and a milk chute. Who can forget the milk chute, where Twin Pines Dairy delivered milk and juice into the side of your house?

I remember my grandfather had cut a square in the side of his garage and then placed a medium sized box inside the garage. This provided a refuge for the dog so she could get out of inclement weather or hot sun. The interior of their house had many beautiful rooms, a large kitchen and dining room with Duncan Phyfe dining set and a door going into the living room and another into the kitchen, a large living room with a French provincial sofa, two large bedrooms downstairs, and a huge upstairs area where I could retreat for peace and serenity.

The bathroom had blue tile with black tile trim. Inside of the medicine cabinet there was a slit built in to dispose of the razor blades that many men used back then.

I remember one day in the summer of 1960, when I was seven years old, standing on a step stool in the bathroom and taking his razor out of the medicine cabinet. My grandfather used a straight razor that opened up when you turned it, and it held a razor blade. I do not really know why, but I decided to shave near my right eyebrow. Being a little kid, I did not realize how sharp the razor was, and before I knew it, I had shaved off the entire eyebrow. By now, my grandfather was knocking on the door as I had locked it. He continued knocking, inquiring, "What is going on in there?" I slowly opened the door, and he looked at me rather quizzically. He never became upset, emotional, or verbally aggressive; he never overreacted. His strong and determined hand gripped mine, and he calmly talked to me about how worried he was—that I could seriously hurt myself if I touched a razor again. He placed a little Band-Aid where my eyebrow had been and told me to have some faith; it would grow back before I knew it.

Neither can I forget the laundry chute located in the bathroom. I remember how clothes would get stuck in it and you had to grab a broomstick and push the stuff down. Around the same time I shaved off my eyebrow, I received a tall, beautiful bride doll from Hudson's from my grandfather. One day I decided to cut off all her hair and afterwards I felt just awful. I thought I would just shove her down the laundry chute, and no one would find out about the "bad hair day." The only problem was that I jammed up the laundry chute at my grandparents' home. I got a scolding for trying to get rid of the evidence, and I also had a fearful thought that no one would buy another doll for me.

Magical Memories

In 1881, Joseph Lowthian Hudson opened his first clothing store located at the Detroit Opera House. Mr. Hudson was born October 17, 1846, in Newcastle-on-Tyne, England and immigrated with his family to Hamilton, Ontario, Canada, when he was nine years old. By age fourteen, he and members of his family were residing in Michigan. In 1881, Mr. Hudson began his store with men's and boys' clothing, and the reasonable prices attracted a lot of customers. Years later, as his business grew, he went on to add women's clothing and house wares. In 1891, his store was incorporated as the J. L. Hudson Company. During the financial panic of 1893, the Third National Bank of Detroit collapsed. Being a generous person and wanting to continue to build interest in his clothing store, Mr. Hudson took personal responsibility for its failure and gave account holders money from his own accounts to match the balances on record. Mr. Hudson's customers remembered his goodwill and all of this was returned to him in the form of an increase in business.

As a child, visiting Hudson's at Christmastime was something that filled me with great joy. This was a fabulous place where I could forget my troubles, at least for a while.

According to Hauser and Weldon in *Images of America: Hudson's, Detroit's Legendary Department Store, 23, 27, 28, 29*

"Everyone in southeastern Michigan knew that the 'real' Santa was ensconced on the twelfth floor of Hudson's. Remember that thrilling express ride on the elevator up to Santaland? Whoosh...past eleven other floors magically filled with holiday décor. It conveyed the magic and merriment of beloved traditions at 1206 Woodward. Legions of families would trek downtown from places near and far, initially by interurban trains and Department of Street Railways streetcars, and later by automobile." Hudson's downtown was known for its prominent window displays, and children in Detroit looked forward to Christmastime and what they could always count on from Hudson's.

There was a distinct difference between the window displays during the early years in Hudson's history and during the fifties and sixties. Hauser and Weldon state, *"During the war years, window displays were less creative due to a shortage of materials. Displays at this time frequently supported the war effort. Interior and exterior holiday lights were dimmed. The 1950s saw a renewed spirit, propelled by a more robust economy and the initial suburban building boom."* What I loved, were the mechanical windows. *"Hudson's legendary mechanical windows featured intricately designed themes that were planned well in advance and in many cases took a year to construct. The bright colors and fanciful imagery they created captivated young and old alike. On weekends, crowds would line Woodward Avenue six deep to catch a glimpse of these creative wonders!"*

**MOTHER WALKING WITH HER CHILDREN DOWN JEFFERSON AVENUE AT CHRISTMASTIME, 1960
(PHOTO COURTESY OF ALAN DENEAU)**

Most baby boomers who grew up in Detroit have their own favorite memories of Hudson's, particularly at Christmastime. I can remember riding in my grandfather's 1960 blue Rambler American with my mother, and circling the Hudson's building. I particularly enjoyed looking at all the animated characters in the store windows. While waiting at the light, a traffic control person was hidden somewhere in the area. If you started to cross the street without waiting in line, you would be startled by a loud voice saying, "Get in line!" As you entered the store, you headed for the elevator, run by a white-gloved elevator operator, who whisked you to the twelfth floor. Hauser and Weldon state, *"Destination Toyland! Was a magical place with hundreds of toys in one room that you could play with. After that you would get in line to see Santa Claus. Before the advent of specialty retailers, Detroiters would not think of purchasing toys, games, puzzles, or dolls from anywhere but 'Hudson's Toy town' on the twelfth floor."*

After visiting Hudson's, we went to well-known places in downtown Detroit, such as Cunningham's for a delicious chicken sandwich or Sanders to enjoy a hot fudge cream puff, and during our drive around the city, were excited to see the Christmas lights at the top of the Penobscot Building.

Hudson's was known for its elegance, beauty and attention to detail particularly during the Christmas season. The images, the simple acts of kindness, the dreams that came to life from the experiences at Hudson's are gifts that elevated everyday life.

**THE GREATER PENOBSCOT BUILDING, 1960, CHRISTMASTIME
(PHOTO COURTESY OF ALAN DENEAU)**

In *The Buildings of Detroit, A History*, Hawkins W. Ferry wrote, *"The forty-seven-story Penobscot Building (1928) was completed on the southwest corner of Griswold and Fort Streets. Dominating the Detroit skyline with its towering bulk, the Penobscot Building was a significant achievement. Emancipated from the shackles of historical styles, it was a bold statement in the language of its day."*

When I became an adult, I learned that because there were so many children and parents coming to see Santa Claus, Hudson's created many lines leading to many rooms where more than one Santa waited. I was grateful when I received new dolls, board games, and art supplies at Christmastime. However, I recall one Christmas, my brother and I received used toys. We did not say anything, but we knew. I received a used doll, and my brother received an old, red metal fire truck. I cried a few tears of frustration, and my brother just pushed the truck aside. My father was laid off from the railroad in 1957, so there was very little money for things like toys. The humorous part about it was we were given Christmas stockings packed with walnuts, oranges, and hard candy. What was I supposed to do with walnuts in the shell? My mother should have included a nutcracker in each stocking. My grandfather came by and gave us each a new book and some clothing for Christmas. In return, we entertained him with funny little stories and soon forgot about the used toys and stretched-out stockings. After we were done entertaining him, we went with him to his house to play with the new, more elaborate Lionel train set he had recently purchased for us. I will never forget playing with the Lionel train he kept set up in the basement.

My grandfather visited our house daily. As a child, I often wondered why my parents found themselves helpless when it came to meeting their parental responsibilities. My parents were continuously calling my grandfather to help them pay the bills, maintain our house, and assist whenever we were ill. They just seemed overwhelmed and overcome with fear of the day-to-day responsibilities of childrearing. Confusion and instability surrounded me most days at my house, but my grandfather's strong presence never wavered and was never far away. My brother and sister benefited from my grandfather's attentions as well. They needed his love, care and guidance too and it was readily available to them.

CHAPTER 5

DARK MEMORIES

I hide myself within my flower,
That wearing on your breast,
You, unsuspecting, wear me too—
And angels know the rest.
I hide myself within my flower,
That, fading from your vase,
You, unsuspecting, feel for me
Almost a loneliness.

—*Emily Dickinson*

I began thinking more and more that there must be something terribly wrong with me, to be placed in such a precarious position, struggling and uneasy as I had to submit to my mother's major depression, psychological delusions, and angry outbursts over and over again. I was the primary casualty of her mental illness as I was the one who was always left alone with her. I often wondered what I had done to cause so much pain and suffering. I was like an innocent bystander, and my conscious mind seemed to be hidden from me. It was like watching me in a movie I didn't want to be in, and no matter what attempt I made to stop it, the movie continued with me as the lead character. The song "Over the Rainbow" sung by Judy Garland in the *Wizard of Oz* was my theme song in my fantasy life. I thought of myself as a good-natured child, loving and deserving of happiness. All I really wanted was a total escape from all the drama.

I began to dread spring because I knew it represented the continuous and ever-present reminder of my mother's unstable state of mind. I knew what lay ahead. I often wondered why I could not pack up and just head over to my grandfather's house and leave all the agony behind. My mother's attention-seeking ways took precedence over anything else going on in my life. When she was on a downward spiral, she would lie on her bed most of the day and request that I sit with her and place a cold compress on her head. I had no other choice but to comply. Even though I was a child, I was expected to assume a parental role.

I will always remember sitting with my mother in her bedroom and listening to her talk to Jesus, who she thought lived in the bedroom closet. She would say to me, "Jesus is in the closet; you can talk to him!" I would reply, "OK, maybe another time." She ranted about how worthless and inadequate she was and she expressed suicidal ideas. She often would remark, "I have nothing to live for." With her sudden mood swings, she could be happy one minute and crying the next.

There would be signs of her yearly downward spiraling: delusional behavior with grandiose ideas, such as Jesus appearing from time to time, telling my mother that she was a famous person, and persecutory delusions, such as strangers trying to destroy her happiness or take her children away from her. Despite all the ways my grandfather tried to help my mother, she viewed her life in a dismal way. No sooner had she achieved some stability and calmness in her daily life, then another spring began, and I witnessed the major depression present itself again.

During this time, Jim was asked by my grandfather to come live with him. I believe my grandfather wanted the company since my grandmother had recently passed away. My father worked long hours and when he was home he had to help take care of my younger sister. I was left to try to care for my mother. I became the one who would have to cope with her mental illness more and more.

This created great anxiety in me and I walked on egg shells. As a child, I believed I had to be careful not to create any negative reactions in my mother or let her emotional reactions snowball. I recall an aunt saying, "Take care of your mother, now."

"It was my responsibility, wasn't it?" The way a child thinks, in a simple manner, I misinterpreted all of this pain, suffering, despair, and tragedy as something I should not doubt but just accept as my fate.

I wondered if it was greedy to hold onto the happy moments I experienced with my grandfather. In looking back at my mother and my grandfather, I see they were profoundly different from one another. June had emotional limitations and was unable to appreciate even the simplest pleasures in life. Robert, in spite of all the tears and adversity, held on to his childlike wonder at life, sense of humor, and gratefulness for each day. My grandfather accepted people in the present tense, with their limitations and abilities. Even though he never talked about it, I sensed he had some difficulty accepting my father's intellectual limitations. My grandfather patiently assisted my father with maintaining a house and paying his bills on a daily basis. My grandfather lived a full life even with all of the painful memories. My mother did not have the awareness that our actions have consequences. She would go from expressing great happiness to sinking into deep depression. I wondered whether she had a genuine desire to die.

I remember feeling at that time that no one understood what I was experiencing, and how could they? I did not talk about it, and there was no counselor, teacher, or therapist to delve into the secrets of my heart. My friends and acquaintances talked about their high grades, their social lives, and their supposedly happy family life. My youth was tarnished with profound mental illness. I was a child, and yet in a detached way, I was expected, by my father, to behave as an adult.

I Stood Alone for a Moment

I learned later through my own personal experience and training as a counselor that trauma affects how children perceive the world around them and other people. The essence of trauma is a sensory experience as a result of what happens to the brain and the memories during trauma. The shame that comes from the trauma leaves a child feeling powerless.

I remember one spring day when I was eight years old more vividly than others. The hands on the clock moved slowly that late afternoon. The intoxicating scents of the early flowers lingered in the air even after their colors had begun to fade. Inside my house the light of day began to disappear before my eyes as early evening approached. As my father busied himself with helping my sister settle down for a nap, I was again alone with my mother. This time, unbeknownst to me, it could have proven to be fatal for me.

I was in my bedroom playing with my dolls when all of a sudden I heard a tapping on my door. It was my crying mother and she wanted my attention. I opened the door and followed her to the other bedroom in the front of the house, my brother's former bedroom. Once again, my mother sought my comfort and wanted me to sit next to her as she rambled from one subject to another, displaying great agitation. I felt scared and utterly alone. I was just a child, and the sudden mood swing and delusional behavior was overwhelming to me. Did I have enough strength to sit beside my mother again and try to comfort her? I tried to minimize the fear I felt and told myself this would pass soon and my father would call my grandfather to inform him of the situation and get my mother to the hospital. Only this time, as I sat next to my mother, she suddenly took a pillow and began to move closely toward my face. It was inconceivable that my mother was trying to suffocate me. But she was.

Frantic, I jumped up. I had to escape! As I instinctively ran into my bedroom, I let out a primal scream. I feared for my life. I screamed to my father, "Call grandfather now!" After I locked myself in the bedroom, I could hear commotion in the house from behind my door but did not dare open the door. The next voice I heard was my grandfather saying, "It's OK now. Open the door, sweetheart. Let's pack up your clothes and get you settled in at grandpa's house." I came closer and closer to the door and finally opened it. I was horrified and in shock. I never told my grandfather about this horrible thing or anyone else until I was much older. My grandfather was talking in a hushed voice, and I was grateful he was there for me again, bringing his compassion and tremendous understanding, as only he could give. The crisis was ending. Once again, the "men in the white coats" came to restrain my mother and transport her to the psychiatric ward in Wyandotte General Hospital.

This was a family matter and was addressed within the family. I remember a lot of secrecy surrounding my mother's depression and consequent hospitalization.

WYANDOTTE HOSPITAL, JULY 2012
(PHOTO COURTESY OF STACEY REYNOLDS)

The events that took place with my mother colored my perceptions and led to my distrust of others, bewilderment, and insecurity. These perceptions shaped my childhood and early adolescence. People diagnosed as mentally ill back in the early 1960s were primarily confined to state institutions or private hospitals—out of sight and out of mind. As a child I had only a vague idea of what was going on in terms of treatment while my mother was hospitalized. Mostly my knowledge came from eavesdropping on telephone conversations between my grandfather and family members on my father's side. Interestingly, I do not recall any telephone conversations occurring between my grandfather, father, and my mother's family.

No matter what I did to try to prepare myself, being told that my mother will be hospitalized for an extended period of time was always a shock. Before I had time to try to wade through it all, I was plunged into a sea of uncertainty and a period of adjustment to living back with my grandfather again. I could confide in my grandfather about my feelings and experiences, but it was only for brief periods of time as he had a lot of responsibilities. During the early 1960s, people did not acknowledge mental illness or those affected by it. My family was no exception to this rule. My grandfather, brother, and father never talked about what was going on in our family, and because of this, my feelings of isolation would return, at least temporarily.

The Physiological Effects of Trauma

Once settled in at my grandfather's house, I would lie on the bed upstairs, staring at the ceiling. I had the sensation that my hands were large. It was the strangest sensation. As a child, I did not know I was experiencing a physiological reaction to the impact of trauma. I experienced traumatic dreams, intrusive thoughts, and anxiety. Between the ages of five and ten, I had trouble sleeping, and was terribly afraid of the dark. I had a reoccurring dream about my entire family, including myself, driving off the Ambassador Bridge.

Trauma and the Impact on the Brain

From my training as a therapist, I learned that the left part of the brain is not fully developed until adolescence is over. Basically, the left and right brain are both affected and are not working together when a child has been traumatized. The left brain cannot make sense of what has happened and has no ability to reason. The neurons in the hippocampus are significantly damaged due to stress hormone release. The hippocampus is where understanding, learning, and processing takes place. Other information gathered from PET scans, or Positron emission tomography, indicate not only is short term memory impaired and learning difficulties occur, but also the trauma affects focusing, attending, and retaining information. The amygdala, also known as the right brain, is the reason why trauma is a sensory experience. Right brain is where trauma is stored. Since trauma is a sensory experience that explains why there are only images, but not words, associated with traumatic memories.

The sensation of my hands feeling large was a sensory experience from trauma. As a child if someone hurt me, I would go into survivor mode. I would be hyper vigilant in my reaction because I could not allow myself to be hurt again. This is where my grandfather created ways to help me shine as a child and try to overcome the trauma. He secured a swing in the basement from the rafters so I could retreat there and have some fun. Did he know this was therapeutic for me? He took me on lots of trips so I could have the experience of seeing new places and engaging with new people. He always encouraged me to draw, which is now one way that is utilized to help a child heal. By communicating on paper, art therapy allows the participant to move from being victim to being a survivor. It also works to help a child communicate on paper what he or she cannot verbalize. It creates a safe place to put the trauma and gives the child a new sense of power and control, along with hope. It certainly did for me.

For the time being, I realized I was safe and the hospital was addressing my mother's depression. As time went by, I became less and less interested in my mother's problems and more interested in what was going on around me at my grandfather's house. I did not want to add to his burdens by complaining. My grandfather did the best he could, but he must have struggled with all the responsibilities that weighed upon his shoulders.

Just like the powerful steam locomotives that brought unlimited vital resources to millions of people, my grandfather was always there bringing comfort, resources, and necessities to me.

Chapter 6

IMAGINATION, OPENNESS AND A LANDSCAPE OF POSSIBILITIES

The source of all humor is not laughter, but sorrow.

—*Mark Twain*

As time passed, and I grew older, I knew the only person I could count on in the long run was I. I realized my grandfather was getting older and even though I desperately wanted everything to remain the same in that I could count on him to always be there for me, I knew deep inside that he would go and I would remain. I decided not to allow anyone to undermine my self-worth or triumphs as I moved forward. I would have to get tough and transform myself from a shy, insecure girl into a whole, balanced person who could weather any storm.

Old Fashioned Speech Therapist

At the age of nine, I was placed in a speech class during regular school hours, three times a week. I had a speech impediment, sticking my tongue out when trying to use words with *s* in them. Miss Goodman, the teacher of the speech class, smelled like lavender soap, wore dark brown and navy suits with shoulder pads, and styled her hair in the Victory roll fashion of the 1940s. She listened carefully to me as I repeated the words she had written on the blackboard beginning with letter *s*. She made me laugh with, "Sam sells seashells down by the seashore." Miss Goodman would always focus on my strengths and reinforce my efforts when I stated words correctly. Miss Goodman could probably see that I had low self-esteem and was fearful about other children teasing me about my speech. What I liked about Miss Goodman was her approach and how she would have all the speech students give her the worst-case scenario concerning their fears. She challenged my fear that other children would imitate me and my speech impediment. I did experience this a few times, so it was a real fear. She suggested that I make up a funny story that would cheer me up when I felt upset by things that others said that were not true. It worked!

Let's Reminisce

Although I was lonely at times, I knew I could create ways to cope with this. Many friends lived near my grandfather's house, and I learned to lighten my mood with my clown-like antics. Many of the kids in my neighborhood entertained one another with self-made stories and jokes. We did not have much money, so I guess we lived in our imagination. We pretended to be in the Detroit Tigers lineup or one of the New York Yankees stepping up to the bat. Most of the parents of the kids I played with were either white-or blue-collar workers, employed with one of the major auto companies, a supplier to the auto companies, or with the state and local government.

I liked making my friends laugh by putting on little skits and plays, starring me of course. I enjoyed putting on puppet shows that were loosely based on *Kukla, Fran and Ollie*, created by Burr Tillstrom. I was also good at standing on my head for long periods of time. I was pleasantly surprised when my peers found my diversions entertaining. My primary goal was to temporarily escape from all the drama that centered on my mother. I was the center of attention, at least for the time being. I found safety in creating funny little plays, all with happy endings, and making others laugh. The children's games and plays became my coping mechanisms for everything I desperately tried to understand.

In the summer of 1962, I rode my shiny, blue bicycle with red streamers on the handle bars and playing cards strategically stuck in the spokes so they made a shuffling noise. I made my way through the neighboring streets in Detroit, which had modest, neat homes with beautifully manicured lawns. While visiting my old chums, I would inevitably get asked about my whereabouts over the past few months. Not wanting my friends to know about my mother's mental illness, I gave a vague answer such as, "Oh, I was visiting family out of state."

My best friend, Linda, would always invite me over to play cutout dolls or tag. Once, as the dinner hour approached, I was invited to stay for dinner and happily accepted. I telephoned my mother and informed her that I would be staying for dinner at my friend's house. She asked when I was coming home and I stated I would be home before the Detroit streetlights came on. She never gave me an argument. I always hung out with my friends at their house as I could not risk inviting chums over and then unexpectedly have to deal with my mother's drastic mood swing. So it was a hardship to never be able to invite friends over. I grew accustomed to going to my friend's homes and playing all day and into the evening, hoping to get invited to spend the night.

The strong bonds I developed and maintained with my friends and their families provided vital ways for me to gain strength, a sense of belonging, safety, security, and love. I was always welcome in their homes and included in birthday parties throughout my childhood. Linda must have informed her mother that I did not have an eighth birthday party. Mrs. Smith surprised me with a birthday party, complete with cake, ice cream, games, gifts, and most importantly friends. Later as I rode my bike home, I cried all the way because I was overcome with gratitude.

Summer Days in Detroit Were Made For This Kind Of Irresistible Fun

Children growing up in Detroit had to use their imagination to find creative, fun things to do. My friend Marty had some short lived success one particularly hot summer. Marty lived in the neighborhood and conspired against the fruits and vegetables man one humid July day. The truck had a green canopy on the side to keep the produce colder. It was like a canvas awning. The fruits and vegetables man was commonly seen driving his little dark green truck through the streets of Detroit all summer long. After observing the fruits and vegetable man for a week, Marty made his move. One day, using a megaphone strategically placed in his bedroom window from the front of his house, Marty, who was mysteriously hidden, began crying out, "I gotta nice fresh strawberries here at only four quarts for a dollar." " Berries, Berries Berries."

In amazement, Marty watched the housewives pour out of their homes and walk toward the street just as the fruit and vegetable man approached in his truck. Suddenly, arguments broke out as the fruit and vegetable man stated, "No! I said I gotta nice, fresh strawberries at three quarts for a dollar."

Marty was succeeding at undercutting the fruit and vegetable man. The neighborhood was in an uproar. This went on for a week until one of the neighbors figured out what was going on and confronted Marty in the window. A police officer visited Marty's parents, Marty's little scheme was exposed to his mother and father, and he was never to be seen or heard from using a megaphone via the bedroom window again.

I often wonder what was going through Marty's mind. Later during that same summer, Marty and his brother, Harold, plotted to throw a dummy that slightly resembled their friend George out of their second-floor bedroom window. On a hot, humid July day, Marty's parents were chatting with the neighbors on the driveway next to their house. Marty and Harold got up their nerve and moved close to the open bedroom window. Neither seemed worried that they may be jeopardizing their upcoming baseball game at Tiger Stadium and the chance to see the Detroit Tigers play the New York Yankees. As they moved the dummy to the edge of the window, they both cried out, "Don't do it, George!" As the dummy dropped to the cement porch below, Marty's mother fainted and was caught by the neighbor who dropped her chi Wawa. Marty and Harold also saw their father look up and without hesitation, stretch out his shaking arms as he prepared to catch the dummy. As Marty's dad realized it was a dummy that he tried desperately to save from destruction, he quickly glanced up to the window on the second floor and saw Marty and Harold laughing hysterically. Marty and Harold's father, Ralph flew up the stairs to the bedroom on the third floor. As Marty and Harold stood there quivering and holding onto each other, Marty said his father pulled his belt out from around his waist and with spit flying out of his mouth, mumbled unintelligible phrases, "How? What have you? What is the matter with you two?" Marty's father was furious; but he had never physically struck either boy before and was not going to then. Both boys were appreciative—they thought that the extent of their punishment was a strong lecture and some additional chores. However, their father informed them they would not be going to the baseball game at Tiger Stadium. Not being able to attend the baseball game at Tiger Stadium proved to be devastating to both Marty and his brother. They waited a long time to go to this game and see one of their hero's play baseball, like the Detroit Tiger Al Kaline.

Of course, my friends who were some of the most beautiful and sweetest kids on earth sat on porch swings, relaxed and listened to the Detroit Tigers play baseball for the rest of the summer. I can still hear the faint echoes of their laughter in my mind.

The Enchantment of Tiger Stadium was not *"Just My Imagination"*, by *the Temptations*

According to *The Corner* authors Richard Bak and Charlie Vincent, *"September 22, 1953, Rookie Al Kaline makes his first start at The Corner, collecting a single while playing centerfield in a 7–3 loss to the St. Louis Browns. On October 31, 1960, forty-five thousand turn out to hear preacher Billy Graham in the largest Protestant rally ever in Michigan. This took place in Briggs Stadium. On April 26, 1960, home run champion Rocky Colavito, acquired from Cleveland in a controversial trade for batting champ Harvey Kuenn, homers in his first Tigers at-bat at Briggs Stadium. On September 10, 1960, Mickey Mantle hits a ball over the right field roof that travels an estimated 643 feet, the longest home run ever measured."*

The End of the Dolls that Sparkled and the Cars of the Future

Another major historic event occurred in Dearborn which is located near Detroit. On November 9, 1962, Linda and I were watching *The Jackie Gleason Show* when the local news broke in with a major story. That Friday, at 1:12 p.m. the alarm had been sounded, and the Ford Rotunda had burned down.

Deneau, stated, *"The Ford Rotunda, built for the 1933 Chicago World's Fair, was taken apart brick by brick, and reconstructed in Dearborn, Michigan. The Ford Rotunda was designed by architect*

Alfred Kahn and opened to the public in June 1953." This was a place where you could see the automobiles of the future. It was lit up all around with colored lights. Remember the Emerald City from the *Wizard of Oz?* This is just what it looked like to a child. The most magical time was at Christmas and Thanksgiving with animated displays of children and animals. Everyone parked in the back and walked up a long walkway. As a child, you were required to hold on to a rope once inside that led you to the attractive displays or you could get lost. The Dolls of the World display was a favorite of mine, and of course, Santa Claus. A place that brought me so much happiness for so long was now gone forever.

**FORD ROTUNDA BURNING, NOVEMBER 9, 1962
(PHOTO COURTESY OF ALAN DENEAU)**

CHAPTER 7

EMBRACING JOY AND DESPAIR

Attitude is a little thing that makes a big difference.

—Sir Winston Churchill (1874-1965)

On my mother's side of the family, there was family reunions going back before I was born, usually held in Three Rivers, Michigan. In the spring of 1963, when I was ten years old, we visited my mother's family in Niles, Michigan. We traveled by train leaving from the Michigan Central Station in Detroit.

In 1913, the Beaux-Arts Michigan Central Station opened in Detroit. It was designed by Warren and Wetmore and Reed and Stem architectural firms who also designed the Grand Central Terminal in New York City. It made all the familiar city and town stops along the way: Ann Arbor, Jackson, Marshall, Battle Creek, Kalamazoo, Decatur, Dowagiac, and lastly Niles. My grandfather told me that, for the most part, the Michigan

Central Railroad operated passenger trains between Detroit and Chicago.

Whimsical Times

I have fond memories of spending time with my aunts, uncles, and cousins. I remember the smell of rose-scented soap and lotion in their houses and the sounds of music playing in the background—songs such as "Enjoy Yourself (It's Later than You Think)," recorded by Guy Lombardo and His Royal Canadians, "Blue Moon," written by Richard Rodgers and Lorenz Hart and "I'll Be Seeing You," written by Sammy Fain and Irving Kahal. All the kids played horseshoes and baseball outside, and one year, my uncle Bob gave all twenty-one of us kids Hula-Hoops. We took them outside and tried to outdo each other by holding a Hula-Hoop contest. Later, my uncle Bob rang the outside bell, and we all ran to the house for corn on the cob, grilled hot dogs, hamburgers, homemade potato salad, and fresh tomatoes from the garden along with peach and apple pie made from scratch. I remember riding horses from neighboring ranches that were fun because they were a bit out of control.

My aunts sang songs like "Smile," written by Charlie Chaplin, John Turner and Geoffrey Parsons and "Catch a Falling Star," written by Paul Vance and Lee Pockriss while they were preparing food for the all-day reunion, and my cousins and I joined in the singing. The day seemed to fly by as we played hide-and-seek well into the evening, with the luminous country landscape in the background and the fireflies starting to make an appearance here and there. The music was sweeter, the food was tastier, the days were longer, and I could feel the joy radiating from all around. It touched me deep inside, and I embraced it.

However, as we were getting ready to leave this family reunion in 1963, the thought of leaving her family triggered another episode of my mother's anxiety and depression. Up until leaving, she had been fine. As I reflect on that trip, I recognize the connection between the grief and loss my mother felt at the end of the reunion and in separating from her family again. She seemed to slip into darkness that was the escape. It is inexplicable as to why my mother again began to slip away from me. I can only guess that the visits to her family must have triggered strong feelings of regret for having moved away and therefore resistance to go back to the responsibilities and life she now had. As we waited for the train at the Niles depot and prepared to return home to Detroit, I could see the beginning of the dramatic emotional and psychological disorientation that would lead to the ensuing breakdown. My grandfather, father, and brother were present. However, they did not seem to notice the de-compensating and depression taking over. Could they have been in denial?

Once home, I immediately noticed the faraway look in my mother's eyes, the unresponsiveness when I asked her a question, the depression consuming her like a dark, ominous storm cloud that comes out of nowhere and changes a precious, bright, sunny day into something to take cover from. Not long after we returned home from the family reunion, my mother rapidly declined and once again was shuffled off to a psychiatric hospital. This time it was Eloise Psychiatric Hospital in Wayne County.

The Unknown and Flickering Memories

My mother was brought to Eloise Hospital this time rather than Wyandotte Hospital because Wyandotte Hospital did not have any beds available.

**ELOISE HOSPITAL, JULY 2012
(COURTESY OF STACEY REYNOLDS)**

I recall very well the day I was taken to Eloise to visit my mother. I don't know whose idea it was for me to stand underneath a window where my mother looked down at me that day. A nurse wearing a white cap was with her as my mother waved to me from the third-floor window. The entire experience had a powerfully negative effect on me. I did not want to be there waving to my mother who was in a dark, depressing psychiatric hospital. I felt angry, sad, and in a strange way, humiliated to see my mother in full view in a window and not be able to talk to her in person. The entire experience had a significant impact on me. I could only stand there frozen in despair, utterly hopeless. I thought it must be a bad dream. I will wake up and none of it will have happened. Unfortunately, it wasn't. It was as intense and painful as any physical problem I could have experienced. My grandfather came up to me and gently guided me away. Afterward, I returned to my grandfather's home, sobbed into my pillow, and prayed for her and myself to be relieved somehow, in some way, of the pain this experience was causing both of us. As an adult, I understand that the behaviors my mother displayed throughout my childhood represented her unmet needs from her childhood. Basically she lacked the ability to adequately communicate her needs through normal verbal means.

According to *A History of the Wayne County Infirmary, Psychiatric, and General Hospital Complex at Eloise, Michigan, 1832–1982*, written by Alvin C. Clark, *"Five years before the State of Michigan was admitted to the Union with a population of 8,800 people, the creation of what was to develop into the Wayne County Infirmary, General, and Psychiatric Hospitals occurred in the City of Detroit on March 8, 1832."*

Maslow's Hierarchy of Needs

In his book *Motivation and Personality*, Dr. Abraham Maslow, the founder of humanistic psychology and the hierarchy of needs, identifies the third area as social needs. Social needs are the needs for belonging, love, and affection. Relationships such as friendships, romantic attachments, and families help fulfill this need for companionship and acceptance, as does the involvement in social, community, or religious groups. I do not see my mother as having succeeded at this level of needs. Due to her emotional problems, she had great difficulty maintaining friendships that generally amounted to no more than having a shoulder to cry on.

As far as going on to the fourth level, the esteem level, my mother never achieved competency at a job and was never recognized for any achievement or success. According to my mother's siblings, her basic needs such as warmth, rest, safety, and security were met for the most part. However, through the Great Depression, my mother's basic need for food was sometimes lacking. Later in life, she seemed obsessed with talking about and obtaining food as evidenced by the daily ritual of walking to the corner A&P grocery store. She was on a first name basis with all the store clerks.

I often wonder about my mother's unmet emotional needs. My mother often complained to me that she did not have emotional support from her family of origin and felt like she did not belong. She stood alone in her family. My maternal grandmother, Cora, did not provide my mother with much one-on-one attention, due to the fact that she had six other children to care for. My maternal grandfather was often away, trying to find work, spending time fixing the house up, or drinking. He was not available to my mother to provide guidance and direction. Her sister, Susan, recalled a childhood incident of out-of-control play that led to my mother getting hit in the head with a hammer. According to my aunt Susan, after this injury, my mother displayed up-and-down moods along with an inability to get along with others at times. This, on top of the head injury she sustained more than likely contributed to her mental illness.

CHAPTER 8

GIFTS AND GUIDANCE FROM ABOVE

In quietness and in confidence shall be your strength.

—Isaiah 30:15

In the fall of 1966, when I was thirteen, I began my classes at Brooks Junior High School in Detroit. Thinking back to my junior high school days, I struggled daily to remain focused and attend school. Everyday my mother tried to prevent me from leaving the house. Her unsuccessful attempts involved becoming overly emotional or depressed as she stated, "I need you here at home." Sometimes she would become angry, and this created feelings of frustration in me. She would insist that I stay home and became argumentative when I challenged her. I walked out the door, and did not look back.

In the 1960s there were no guidance counselors to provide specialized services and interventions to students experiencing trauma or neglect in their home environments. My school counselor was available to assist students only with their schedule or when they got into trouble at school. I did not feel comfortable going to the counselor to discuss my family dysfunction. In the 1970s the developmental/preventive models came along, and in 1979 the American School Counselor Association adopted this approach. The principles of the developmental/preventive models are developmental guidance and counseling which helps students cope with issues and problems that are normal to growing up and becoming adults. It considers the nature of human development, including the general stages and tasks of normal maturation, and encompasses three approaches: remedial, crisis, and preventative.

After telling my mother I was intent on getting an education, I then decided I had to depend upon myself. I had to gather up all the strength within me and have faith in my heart. As strange as it sounds, at that same moment I also heard a voice inside of me telling me to embrace all the hopelessness and despair, "God will pull you through it."

For the next few years, almost every day I was late for Mr. Carlin's daily homeroom class. He would hold me back from going to my first class for being late. Mr. Carlin would instruct me to write out on a piece of paper fifty times, "I will not be late for homeroom class." Either it never occurred to him to inquire why I was late so often, or he just did not want to get involved. He never knew what an enormous struggle it was for me just to get to school or exactly what it meant to me to have some peace for a while.

Developing Resiliency

As time went by and I developed new friendships at school, I became adept at protecting my own mental health and flourished. As an adolescent, I loved art class: drawing and other creative pursuits let my imagination carry me away. It became too difficult to constantly stay on the defensive, so I would masquerade as a comedian, even acting as the class clown at times. Mr. Johnson, our eighth grade math teacher, had a dark brown liquor bottle in his desk drawer. One day, before Mr. Johnson arrived to start the class, I sat in his big, black chair that swiveled around. He had a rather nasally, high-pitched voice that was easy to imitate. In the big, black chair, I recited some recent homework assignments while I pulled the bottle of liquor out of the drawer and pretended to be drinking it.

One of my fellow classmates jumped up and looked down the hall and yelled loudly, "Here he comes!" I jumped out of the big, black chair and ran to my seat. What I did not realize was that I was beginning to develop a stronger sense of humor and resilience. I learned about building strong friendships with the girls that I went to school with, while we all danced to the Rolling Stones, set our hair in huge rollers, and smoked cigarettes when their parents were not around. Through these loving, beautiful relationships, I caught a glimpse of how many families live in a positive light, and it helped me to start healing.

In high school, I often had a feeling of hopelessness and would sometimes feel resigned to the experience of being trapped by the circumstances revolving around my mother. I had to find an escape and began hanging out with my friends at their houses on a daily basis. I was accepted by my peers, and this helped me tolerate an intolerable situation with my mother. I began to attend a church group for teenagers that met twice a week at Grandale Presbyterian church on Plymouth Road. It provided a safe and friendly atmosphere where adolescents could come together to participate in a sports activity, join a Bible discussion group, or just talk freely without worry about being judged. The program was facilitated by the assistant pastor and a camp coordinator, who was also a counselor. Ongoing weekly meetings helped me to develop strengths such as self-reflection and problem-solving skills.

I wish I could forget these upcoming events, but I cannot. Resilience is the ability to adjust to special problems and achieve positive outcomes. I had never had a boyfriend before. Looking back now, I believe I fell in love because I was so impressed with his good looks and the attention he was bestowing upon me; I was intrigued with this mysterious nineteen-year-old man I hardly knew.

A lack of Awareness

One day John magically materialized and started attending the youth group activities. Right away, he started showing a strong interest in me. Having low self-esteem at that time, I was very flattered by all the attention. I was only fifteen, and I could not muster up the strength or wisdom to resist him. John called me every day and gave me a ride home from the church. John and I went to the movies and restaurants; we visited his parents' home three to four times a week. I had no guidance or concern from my parents, and my grandfather was advancing in years. I confused sex with love and one night found myself alone at his parents' home with just John. I was not making decisions from a place of awareness or consciousness. I was so desperate for love and attention that I could not conceive of any other life except one where I would be struggling. Before long, I gave into John's advances. Emotionally I felt very vulnerable and scared. I wondered how I could have let something like this happen. Within two months, I was aware of the fact that I was pregnant. I could not tolerate being in school anymore. I was experiencing severe morning sickness, which made it impossible to be there and try to focus on my studies.

I told John that I was pregnant and he said, "We will get married." By this time John had been drafted by the army and was already in Fort Knox, Kentucky starting his basic training. Every day I wondered how or when I would be able to tell my parents, my grandfather, and my boyfriend's parents.

I was sixteen years old in March 1969 when I finally decided to inform everyone that I was pregnant. I had hidden the fact that I was five months pregnant well with baggy clothing. I had experienced great criticism from my mother for most of my life when it came to circumstances that required compassion. My mother did not respond to life's changes and transitions in a normal way, and as expected, she overreacted when I told her I was pregnant. She said, "I should disown you! What will the neighbors think?" I was now faced with circumstances that were frightening, powerfully illuminating, and ultimately transforming. In retrospect, now I can see the ridiculousness of my mother's statement. My reaction to her statement should have been, "What do the neighbors have to do with my life—the goals, direction, and future of it?" When I looked at my father after he had been told the news, he had tears in his eyes and was silent.

As I waited for my grandfather to come over so I could tell him of the pregnancy, I was fearful that he would be so emotionally hurt that he would not be able to offer the guidance that he had provided most of my young life. Would my grandfather be the one person who would offer understanding and compassion?

After I broke the news to him, in his most compassionate, gentle way, he spoke to me in that calm, reassuring voice that I knew so well, "We will take care of that little girl together." I have no idea how he knew the baby was a girl, but I completely trusted his words. I discovered within myself the ability to keep moving forward, believing that with God's help I had everything I needed to face the challenges that lay ahead. I refused to become depressed and began to plan for my future and prayed for the spiritual guidance and power that would be required for me to succeed in handling the tasks before me.

While visiting my grandfather, I received a phone call from John. He wanted me to buy a roundtrip Greyhound bus ticket and come to Fort Knox by the weekend so we could get married. John stated the law for getting married in Kentucky was different than Michigan, and the fact that I was sixteen years old was not a problem. He assured me that his sergeant would be present as a witness at the courthouse in Elizabethtown, Kentucky. John had already looked into the marriage license issue, and he indicated we could obtain that prior to the ceremony on the same day. No one supported our decision to get married. My mother managed to turn the focus on her and how my pregnancy was affecting her life in the neighborhood and the imagined gossip it was creating. My father went to work and did not say a word about the upcoming nuptials. My grandfather had no opinion on marriage, and my brother wisely advised that I did not have to get married if I did not want to.

So at the age of sixteen and pregnant, I made the decision to travel to Kentucky to marry my boyfriend. I packed a little green suitcase and took a yellow cab to the bus depot in downtown Detroit. I purchased my roundtrip ticket and boarded the bus for Fort Knox, Kentucky. I sat in the last seat, feeling scared but not moving. I studied people's faces on the bus, looking for friendly expressions. I did not find any. I recalled the passage from the Bible, Psalm 46:1, *"God is our refuge and strength, a very present help in trouble."* I prayed to God, "Please walk with me in this difficult time." I was moved by a force that came to me as I focused on this passage as the bus pulled out of the Greyhound bus depot and accelerated on the freeway heading south. Something profound happened to me that night, and I had a new sense of purpose. I realized that it was not about me anymore, I had a child on the way and it added great power to my growing inner strength.

Learning to rely on Faith and Spirituality

On May 31, 1969, John and I were married. We arrived at the courthouse, which was situated in the middle of Elizabethtown,

Kentucky. We were rushing to get there before they closed the doors for the day, and just as we arrived, the county clerk was about to lock the door. We pleaded with him not to and informed him this was the only chance we had to get married. As I stood there trembling, the clerk opened the door and ushered us upstairs. The county clerk took information from us and typed up the marriage license. We proceeded into the judge's chamber, along with John's sergeant and the county clerk. The judge opened a small book and began, "John, will thou have this woman to be thy wedded wife, to live together in the holy estate of matrimony? Wilt thou love her, comfort her, honor and keep her, in sickness and in health and forsaking all others keep thee only unto her, so long as you both shall live?" John answered yes. And when it was my turn to answer these questions, I answered yes, and away we went back to military guesthouse quarters for one night together. I felt relieved and happy because I knew I did the right thing. During the middle of the night, I became violently ill, vomiting all night. Sufficc to say, it wasn't much of a honeymoon.

Two o'clock the next afternoon, my new mother-in-law, Joan, showed up at the guesthouse. It seems she had driven there as fast as she could to confront us and try to convince us this was all a big mistake. She did not want her son to marry me and a few weeks earlier had made an attempt to convince me to give the baby up for adoption. She even took me to a girl's home for unwed women in a nearby county and claimed we were visiting a relative. I informed her I was not giving up my child for adoption. I could not wonder my entire life where my daughter was and what she was doing. So I was not surprised when she showed up after we were married. Joan wanted us to get the marriage annulled immediately and wait until after the child was born to get remarried so she could throw us a big, lavish wedding. This plan lacked credibility. John did not want any part of this plan and neither did I. Joan insist that I return to Detroit with her. I was silent most of the trip back, and John went back to his base to complete his basic training.

On July 17, 1969, I called my grandfather, and he sent my brother, Jim to pick me up at three thirty in the morning from my parent's house on a sweltering, humid night with a temperature of ninety-eight degrees. My parents did not even get up when Jim arrived to take me to the hospital. We drove to the Wayne State University campus area in Detroit, in search of Brent General Hospital. We circled a building that turned out to be a college dorm. It looked like a hospital except it had no large sign or entrance to indicate that. After a few minutes of circling, I said, "The hospital must be on a different street; let's get the heck out of here!" Finally, we found the little hospital and entered. I inquired at the front desk about a wheelchair, and the nurse on duty stated, "No, there aren't any available." The next thing I knew, I was following a large, older, female nurse with a heavy German accent, wearing a starched white cap, white uniform, hose, and shoes down a long white corridor. She directed me to remove my clothes and put the hospital garb on. The only other thing she said was, "The hospital is under construction, and there is no air conditioning."

I followed the nurse's instructions and lay on the gurney. The labor pains were pretty intense by that time and coming regularly. I was left alone in that hospital labor room with an occasional visit from a nurse to check on me. If there was a time, more than any other, when I had benefited from memorizing Bible passages, it was now. I remembered Psalm 121:1, *"I will lift my eyes up to the hills from whence comes my help."*

My daughter, Kelly, was born on July 17, 1969. With just one look, I was mesmerized. I knew my purpose was to provide a safe and happy home for my child. My grandfather was the first visitor. With tears in his eyes, he came to me, swept Kelly up in his strong arms, and enthusiastically said, "She has made such an impression on me, and we just met!" I said, "This is just the beginning!" We both laughed. Other family members streamed in for over eight solid hours. I wish I could say that my mother was present, but she missed this watershed event in my life. The truth is she had scheduled a small cyst to be removed from her finger the day that I was due to have the baby. This was to become a pattern for her over the years ahead. At every major life event of mine, my mother was absent. Before leaving the hospital, my grandfather offered his home to me and the baby. So when it was time to leave, Kelly and I went to live with my grandfather. John was able to come home for a brief military leave of absence to meet his daughter, and I began my recovery.

Romantic Love

October 1969 came with its bold red and gold colors, cooler nights, and wild wind that took a hold of you as you walked down the street. John was not in the military long, when it became apparent to the military doctors that he had serious psychological problems. He was diagnosed with major depression, and the remainder of his time was spent at an army hospital located in Fort Riley, Kansas. I suspected something was wrong with John, but being so young and naïve, I could not be sure if he suffered from major depression like my mother had or something else. It was a sad irony because I had started feeling more and more like all the problems I coped with related to my mother were remote now. John was sent to the army hospital for observation and to await discharge. Per John's request, I visited him at Fort Riley and for a few weeks stayed in the guesthouse, which was near the hospital. Having made amends with my mother-in-law, she cared for our daughter while I was visiting John.

I walked over to the hospital every day to visit not only John, but the many soldiers who had recently returned from Vietnam. As a young person who had never traveled far from Michigan or from my family, it was a very humbling experience for me. I deliberately set about every day to visit each ward, in an effort to talk and listen to each person as they shared their experiences, feelings, sorrows, and hopes. Soldiers grasped my hand. Some were blind, and many were missing limbs, but I witnessed all of them light up and become alert as I made my way through the hospital wards letting them know I was thinking of them and praying for them and that a higher power was accessible and they could rely upon it. One soldier named David, who told me he had grown up in the inner city of Detroit, caught my attention. He always wanted to play Scrabble, and I indulged him by playing for over two hours a day. David was a lieutenant who had served two years in Vietnam. He had rescued four men out of his platoon during a siege through Laos into South Vietnam. David told me when he was eight years old, his mother was institutionalized for schizophrenia, and his father had passed away. He was placed with relatives near Lansing and grew up on a farm. Although not his biological parents, he said growing up with his aunt and uncle helped him to grow and heal through all of his grief. He said he learned that he was a part of something bigger than himself; he learned to succeed through hard work, to focus his attention on the little joys in life, and to be thankful for every day. David told me he felt proud to have had the opportunity to serve his country. Listening to David, I realized we both shared a self-awareness that connected us to a higher power and a deeper understanding of ourselves.

Part of each day was spent visiting my husband or playing cards and talking with other soldiers in the same ward. John and I befriended Bill, the soldier in the bed next to John's. Bill was a sergeant who was recuperating from an accident involving an ax and the Boy Scouts. The sergeant had taken a troop of Boy Scouts on an outing in the woods and accidently cut his foot with an ax. Bill was talkative, outgoing, friendly, and much older than my husband and shared lots of stories from his military career and tours of duty. We trusted him.

Apparently, Bill filed the fact that I was staying at the guesthouse in his mind. I awoke one night at two o'clock to the most frightening clamor outside of my door. Someone was trying to force his way into my room, banging and pulling on the door relentlessly. As I sat upright in bed, scarcely able to move, I remembered that I had turned the bolt and put the chain on the lock before retiring for the night. Finally the person gave up. I heard footsteps across the corridor floor and the door slam shut. Wiping the frost off the window, I slowly looked out and saw a man, sporting a brush cut and short in stature, walking quickly down the sidewalk and toward the parking lot. Surprisingly, the figure looked like Bill. How clever of him to deceive us. The next day I informed John of what had taken place, and he was furious. We immediately requested a room change to the main guesthouse. I felt safe at the main guesthouse as it had a great amount of activity going on since the laundry room, TV room, and a kitchen were located in that building. We were able to discern that the sergeant had been discharged from the hospital the day before this incident took place. No one seemed to know where the sergeant had gone. I felt betrayed and angry.

Soon after this incident, I became aware of a young man by the name of Andy. Andy was a Vietnam veteran awaiting discharge, and he made the rounds to the wards on a daily basis, connecting with the patients for brief periods of time. John indicated that Andy was a drug dealer. I do not know where Andy obtained his drugs, but he had drugs that were readily available for whoever wanted them. John told me Andy offered him anything he wanted, but he declined the offer. Months later, after John was discharged, I found pills in John's dresser drawer. I asked what they were and never got an explanation from him. This was the beginning of what would become John's major dysfunction and addiction to drugs. Prior to this period of time John never took or used any substances.

John was discharged from the military in March 1970 and returned home. With the help of my grandfather, John began working for the New York Central railroad in May 1970. I was adapting to motherhood and its inherent responsibilities. I also sought out a tutor to assist me in preparing to obtain my high school diploma. After a short time, I obtained my high school diploma and began thinking about going to college. My grandfather secured a good job for John as a switchman, and for a while he was a dependable worker. However, after three years of dependability, John began to miss work. I should have seen the signs that our marriage was in trouble. John often disappeared for long periods of time and lied about attending to his job responsibilities, and I often found drug paraphernalia in the house or in his car. He would lie to me and his supervisor as to his whereabouts when he was supposed to be working. His good friend Richard called me on the phone one particular August night in 1973 and said that John was involved with another woman. I thought John was on an extended job for the railroad, which took him out of town over a weekend. According to Richard, this had been going on for some time. I was furious! At first I did not want to believe Richard and told him so. But after hanging up, I realized it was the truth, and I had to accept it, have a good cry, face it, and begin the process of moving forward with my life. This reminded once again that to get through the darkness I had to gather up all the courage inside me I could find and use it as my fortress. The difference this time was that, instead of praying for a savior to help rescue me, I had to become my own savior. Even through many lonely days and nights, I held on to the belief that life was still good and began to call upon the friends I had made. For the first time in my life, I began to see each challenge as a part of the learning process for life.

I knew our marriage was over the night John threw one of his black army boots at my head and knocked me out cold. The situation with John had become intolerable. I had become a victim of domestic violence. John had a 1972 brown Corvette parked in the garage. I threw all of his clothing, personal items, and music tapes into the Corvette. Needless to say, it was jammed full of his personal belongings. When he finally came home, late on a Sunday night from his so-called extended work responsibility, I was sitting in the living room, waiting for him. I had rehearsed everything I was going to say to him. John unlocked the front door and walked in to the living room, and he jumped when he saw me. There I was, sitting in the dark, just waiting to confront him on his sins. John asked me, "What are you doing sitting here in the dark?" I replied, "You are leaving, and I have put all of your things out in the Corvette." John replied, "I am taking my stereo with me too!" And I replied, "You can have custody of the drapes if you like—just get out!" I called my grandfather and he offered his home to my daughter and me. My grandfather was advancing now in years, but provided the same compassion and understanding as he had in the past. I filed for divorce in September 1973 and gained full custody of our daughter. Due to the no fault law just going into effect, two years passed, until finally I was a free woman.

Moving Ahead

After the divorce I worked fulltime as a secretary, assistant bookkeeper, assistant office manager, and typist in order to support Kelly and myself. My mother lived on St. Mary's Street with my father, who was in poor health. She had difficulty coping with the challenges my sister faced, being mentally challenged herself. My mother called everyday seeking my grandfather's help with my sister. My grandfather, well into his eighties now could only listen to my mother and try to offer easy solutions to her dilemmas. I visited my mother occasionally. I realized the longer I stayed away, I found more strength and peace within myself.

In addition to working fulltime for two Insurance Companies from 1972 through 1977, I began taking some basic business courses in the evening at Henry Ford Community College. I moved to Ann Arbor in the fall of 1978 and began courses in child psychology at Washtenaw Community College. Kelly and I lived in a co-op house owned by the University of Michigan and set up strictly for couples with children, single parents with children, and one studio apartment for a couple. Being a co-op, each person had a responsibility as an officer. I was the secretary and the maintenance person. I ensured a garden was planted and cared for, mowed the lawn, and fixed minor maintenance problems in the house.

A Case of Bullying

Kelly was in the fourth grade and attended one of the local elementary schools. One day she told me a male student was bullying her as she waited for the bus in front of the school at the end of the day. I contacted her teacher, Mr. Hawkins, and had a consultation with him regarding the student who was bullying my daughter. Mr. Hawkins indicated he would contact the parents of the boy and inform them of what had been going on. I heard back from Mr. Hawkins a few days later, and he assured me that the parents were addressing this with their son. However, the bullying continued over the next couple of weeks. Kelly would come home crying every day and report how she was bullied by this boy again. Once again, I contacted the teacher, and once again he indicated he would address this issue with the parents. Another week went by, and the bullying continued. One day, Kelly returned home from school, upset and crying that the boy was still harassing her by pushing her and making mean statements, such as, "You are stupid; you don't belong here, and you are a slouch." I stated, "That is it! I will insist upon a meeting with the parents of the boy bullying you, your teacher and you and me." Kelly was happier in the days ahead, and when I inquired about the bully, Kelly stated, "My teacher informed me that a meeting is scheduled in three days. When I told the boy about this, he rode away crying on his bike and has not bothered me since!" My wish was achieved through diplomatic, rational means.

Moments that Move Me

By the beginning of 1979, my ex-husband had gotten remarried. He had married Marilyn, with whom he had a love affair with in high school. Marilyn was a tall, attractive blond, ballroom dancer with the popular Arthur Murray dance school. I would later learn from my former mother-in-law that the marriage was on the rocks, and within six months of them getting married, Marilyn was contemplating divorce. In the fall of 1979, Kelly and I were living in Ann Arbor. I had just completed my first semester at Eastern Michigan University after completing two successful semesters at Washtenaw Community College. On December 20, 1979, I received a phone call at six in the morning from my former mother-in-law. Joan called to inform me that John had passed away earlier that morning. He was thirty. She did not have all the details of the circumstances surrounding his death, but they were suspicious. Marilyn had found John in the bathtub, lying in a few inches of water. In addition to informing me of John's death, Joan indicated that a few days before he died, he had been in an altercation with a guy. Joan stated that the guy attacked John, hitting him in the head. Not long after this occurred, Joan said, John came to her house, and she noticed he had blood in his ear. Joan urged John to go to the hospital, but he refused. Later, Joan informed me that the county coroner's examination indicated that the first cause of death was drowning and the second cause of death was cerebral anoxia, a lack of oxygen to his brain. This was puzzling, yet a subsequent police investigation did not identify any other determination for the cause of death. An autopsy was conducted, and it confirmed that John did have a history of narcotic use. After some discussion with my former mother-in-law, she maintained that John had recently confided to her that he found evidence in his house linking Marilyn romantically with another man. Coincidentally, the week before John's death, John confronted Marilyn of his suspicion that she was having an affair. I was extremely saddened by this entire series of events, but at the same time, I knew I had to be strong and hold it together for my daughter, Kelly.

Looking back, the funeral plays like a movie in slow motion. I never received any financial support from John or any parenting support. I realized a long time ago that I was the parent who would have to assume complete responsibility for my daughter and in meeting her needs. As I walked into the funeral parlor holding my daughter's hand I felt completely alone. Even though I consciously knew John never was much of a father to my daughter, it still created in me a deep sadness, and I felt as if the muscles in my legs went limp. With physical support from my former father-in-law, I walked up to view the body of the person I once loved and was married to. This was an unforgettable experience for me. I remember looking into the coffin and seeing John wearing a white suit, white vest, black shirt, and black tie. John looked like he was dressed to go to a disco rather than be buried.

The next thing I recall, I was sitting at a desk along with the funeral director, who was an older, small, plump man with very thick glasses. In a very calm manner, he explained to me that I was now eligible for social security benefits along with Marilyn. He explained he would start the process of submitting the required documentation and urged me to immediately sign the forms he placed in front of me. I signed them and drove home in a relentless rain storm. I did have some feelings of relief at having some of the financial burden lifted from me. At the age of twenty-six and with the help of my brother and sister-in-law steadying me, I buried my old feelings of anger and resentment along with my ex-husband.

CHAPTER 9

OUT OF TRAGEDY COMES NEW HOPE

Every great dream begins with a dreamer. Always remember, you have within you the strength, the patience, and the passion to reach for the stars to change the world.

—*Harriet Tubman*

Submitting to feelings of self-pity would not provide me with the strength, wisdom, power, and resolve I needed to move forward and mature into a positive role model for my daughter. Through my tears and heartbreak, I prayed for God to surround me with his love and mercy and walk with me into the unknown. Within six weeks of John's funeral, my father passed away after a massive heart attack.

I never got a sense of whom he was or what he thought about. The only memorable experience I have of spending time and doing something fun with him was when he took my brother and me sledding at Edward Hines Park in the winter. My eyes filled with tears as I let go of a connection to my father.

My father's body was in the Wayne County morgue located in downtown Detroit. It was up to me to identify his body and inform my ninety-three-year-old grandfather that his only child had passed away. It proved to be one of the most difficult things I ever had to do. I walked down into the dark, cold corridor towards the door identified as the morgue. A young African-American male assistant to the Coroner opened the door and led me to drawer. He pulled it open and I saw my father lying there, cold and barely recognizable. I thanked the young assistant and left. Now I hurried back to my grandfather's house. He was visiting the neighbor, so I walked over to Mrs. Powers' house. As soon as my grandfather saw me he jumped up and asked me "What was wrong?" I replied in the gentlest manner I could, "Grandfather, Dad is gone; he passed away two hours ago." My grandfather began crying and then stumbled out the front door. He ran to his house and I ran after him. He repeated over and over, "It can't be true, God took him before me?" He found some photo albums and began going through them, pointing out baby pictures and happier times. For so many years he was my strength and my voice. Now I became his. I will never forget that night.

Voices Emerge from the Past

In November 1981, I received the phone call I dreaded would come. Up to this time my grandfather lived on his own in his home in Detroit. Recently he had been experiencing some health problems related to the urethra. The medication administered was not working. Eight days before Thanksgiving, my grandfather had been taken to Botsford Hospital with a blockage in the urethra and would require immediate surgery.

My grandfather was then ninety-four years old, but I always thought of him as full of life, energized and strong. Shortly after arriving at the hospital, I visited with my grandfather in the pre-surgical room. Once again, I witnessed his great sense of humor and faith in a higher power as he comforted us. He was aware that Kelly was in the waiting room as she held a marvelous place in his heart. They had a close relationship because we lived with him for a while when she was small, and she was the first great-grandchild. Kelly was too young to be allowed into the area where he was resting before his surgery. Unbeknownst to me, before we arrived my grandfather had told the doctors and nurses monitoring him that my daughter was older than she actually was. So, for twenty minutes my daughter sat next to her great-grandfather and talked about what she did in school that day, the fun things she participated in at camp Algonquin on Burt Lake over the summer, and learning to speak Spanish. Then it was time for her to say good-bye. The doctor informed us that due to my grandfather's advanced age, he could have a massive heart attack during the surgery or after. The doctor asked again, "Do you understand the possible consequences of the surgery?" My grandfather indicated he did and stated to the doctor, "The Lord is with me; I am not afraid."

Anxiously my family and I waited for news from the doctor. The doctor walked toward us, very solemn, and told us that my grandfather had had a heart attack shortly after the surgery and was not expected to live very long. The doctor urged my brother and me to visit with him since he was conscious. I stood by his bed and told him how grateful I was for the love, encouragement, inspiration, and faith that he instilled in me. I thanked him for being there for me and through so many of my struggles. My words did not seem sufficient enough. He deserved so much more. I saw his eyes blink several times, telling me he understood what I said, and then his eyes closed as he slipped into unconsciousness. My grandfather, inspiration and friend, died on November 20, 1981. I was devastated. How could I bear this loss of the one person who knew me so well and loved me unconditionally with all my faults? I sat in my old car, with the rain pouring down outside, and went back in time to try to recall places and feelings from the past life I lived with him. One of the first memories I have of my grandfather was his daily determination to get me to smile when he came to my house on St. Mary's. He was always urging me to never be a stick-in-the-mud. I think he meant for me to be enthusiastic, creative, and imaginative and to take the lead whenever I could. These may be simple thoughts, but they carry a powerful message. By living one's life through connections with others in an authentic, enthusiastic, imaginative, and determined way, it is possible to overcome tragedies and circumstances that seem beyond our control.

Later in the evening, I stopped by his house in Detroit just to walk through the house and look at some old photographs. I noticed his best black suit, black tie, black socks, white shirt, and black shoes placed neatly on the bed. He knew what lay in front of him and was prepared emotionally and spiritually. After the funeral, Robert Frederick Williams was laid to rest in late November 1980 at Forest Hill Cemetery in Ann Arbor next to my grandmother and my father.

Despite my grief, I continued with my art history classes and sought employment, knowing my grandfather would have wanted me to. I was living in Ann Arbor during my late twenties, growing intellectually, emotionally, and spiritually. Making friends always came easily to me, and I had a strong sense of belonging during my college days. I was able to follow up on my assignments and chores and managed to juggle all the odd jobs I had.

Time to go to Work

One odd job I held was as a "clicker" for a New York–based company. They mailed me my instructions, which informed me to be present at the movie theater entrance and count the number of adults and children prior to entering the theater. One evening I decided to treat my daughter to a night at the movies. Unbeknownst to me, the movie they were playing was about gangsters and not age appropriate, and we left immediately.

I had many friends in Ann Arbor during the 1980s, and I informed them I would work cleaning homes. Within a month I had three cleaning jobs working for wealthy families, along with a variety of other odd jobs I picked up along the way. I was asked once by one of the ladies that I cleaned for if I had experience serving catered food. I assured her that, yes, I had lots of experience coordinating large events and parties. Of course, I had no experience doing this type of work. When she called, I scribbled down the time and date of the party and that I was to wear a basic black-and-white outfit. I arrived early and began organizing each plate, complete with potatoes, carrots, and beef Wellington. Each beef Wellington had each guest's initials on it. It was the hit of the evening, and I was a great success.

I greatly enjoyed the classes in art history until one day when a fellow student stated, "You will have to complete a PhD in art history to secure a job." I thought seriously about what she said and decided to switch my major to counseling. I saw a connection between choosing counseling as a means to understand my mother, my childhood, and as a way to help others. I continued my cleaning jobs because, by this time, I was an expert at it.

Along with cleaning homes and attending classes, I secured a position in housing at Eastern Michigan University. I was the assistant manager for the four-hundred-unit family housing apartment complex on campus. After interviewing for the job, the housing manager called me and asked, "How about starting Monday at eight thirty?" "That is fine," I replied, "and can you tell me how much I will be making an hour?" The housing manager replied, "Four dollars and seventy-five cents an hour." I tried to wrangle for more money, but this went nowhere. I was enthusiastic about my job because I could work independently, and it provided me with time to type my papers for my graduate classes. I thought to myself, "This will be a breeze!" Little did I know!

When I arrived for work on Monday, I was handed a tall stack of work orders. Maureen, a stocky woman with red hair, a lovely smile, and a New Jersey accent, who was the apartment manager for the complex, indicated there was a backlog of apartments with problems, such as plumbing, holes in walls, and various other issues. I stated I would take care of them, having not even seen the apartments. Just then the phone rang, and Maureen said, "Oh, that phone is so annoying!" Shortly after taking the phone call, Maureen said, "I will see you later today." I did not see her again for over three weeks. I was determined to do a good job and see to it that tenants had their housing needs met. After tackling the tall stack of work orders, I followed up on every call that came in for backed-up toilets, noisy neighbors, carpet removals, carpet replacement, painting, patching holes in walls, trashed apartments, and tenants parking in parking spots not assigned to them.

The drama at work followed me home to the apartment complex where I lived. The complex I lived at had no assigned parking places, and students could park wherever they wanted. One day, as I was returning from class, I parked closer to my apartment building than I usually did. As I made my way to my apartment, I noticed a couple of guys standing close to the apartment building, talking to each other. One of the guys said to me, "You can't park there; that is my spot." At first I thought he was kidding. Suddenly I realized he was not by the look on his face. I said, "There are not assigned parking places here; this is a free country, and people can park wherever they want." I had a gut feeling that this guy was not going to let this go, but I chose to continue to walk home. The next day, as I left to attend my classes at seven thirty in the morning, I tried to open my car door, but the lock appeared to be jammed. I tried to open all of the doors, and all the locks were jammed, with the exception of the hatchback lock. I was able to open it and climb in through the back. Whoever pulled this prank got a big laugh knowing I had to crawl through the back of the car to get in. I decided to avoid future problems with this neighbor and did not park in that spot again. After all, I had greater demands on my time now.

I realized my GPA was not anything to write home about. After completing my bachelor's degree, I had serious doubts as to whether I possessed the potential to continue on toward a master's degree, which was my great dream. With a lot of encouragement from my friends and my daughter motivating me, I decided to pursue my dream. I had overcome the shyness and low self-esteem I struggled with as a child and believed through my strong faith in God and in myself that I would triumph over any future obstacles and challenges.

In June 1983 I had an appointment with the head of the counseling department so he could advise me on the graduate program curriculum. I presented myself in a positive and distinctive manner, explaining with great enthusiasm that I wanted to enter the master's program in counseling. The advisor was not impressed. He proceeded to remind me of my low GPA as an undergraduate student and insisted I would never be successful in completing the master's program. He gave reasons for why I should "just put the entire idea" out of my mind. I owe him a lot because it provided me with tremendous determination and fortitude to prove him wrong. I asked for one chance to complete four graduate classes while on probation and achieve high grades. He did agree to this and added once again, "It does not matter; you will fail." I took the challenge and completed the courses with high grades. I requested a new advisor and was taken off probation. I registered for my next semester and went on to complete my master's degree program. I could hear my grandfather's words in my ear, "The world is waiting for you; give the world the best you have to give; believe in God and believe in yourself."

Even though my grandfather was gone, his strong influence came into play. This memory was crucial for me in becoming a productive and positive adult. I realized as an adult, I am a person who is productive and capable of making my own strong connections to the world around me.

Throughout my life, my grandfather is still always there by my side, guiding me. I believe this is true in good and in bad times. My grandfather lifted my spirit more times than he was ever aware of. He came to me with a positive attitude, listened to me, and provided stability and guidance. He succeeded in protecting me from the gossip and negative remarks about my mother. He took care of me when I was sick and provided learning activities that a child needed to develop and grow. Many of my most cherished memories are the times I spent with my grandfather.

Chapter 10

FIGHTING BACK WITH RESILIENCE

If I were to try to read, much less answer, all the attacks made on me, this shop might as well be closed for any other business. I do the very best I know how—the very best I can; and I mean to keep doing so until the end. If the end brings me out all right, what's said against me won't amount to anything. If the end brings me out wrong, ten angels swearing I was right would make no difference.

—Abraham Lincoln

My mother lived in northwest Detroit in my grandfather's house for a few years during the 1980s until the day she heard someone trying to get into the side door of the house. She called the police, but it took a while for them to arrive. Meanwhile, the home invader made his way inside and grabbed my mother's purse. She hid but he found her. She told him the police were on the way. He was not inside the house long when the

Detroit police arrived, and then he took off running. Shortly after the robbery, my mother moved in with my sister.

During the middle 1980s and into the 1990s, while I attended college, and then began working, my mother primarily lived with my sister, Carol, in southwest Detroit. I visited my mother at least once a month while she was living with my sister. They lived in a Detroit neighborhood that was rather run down and known for crime and poor housing conditions. They all moved to an old apartment over the top of a bar in a drug-infested neighborhood, complete with boarded up houses and drug deals transpiring in the street. Many years later, my sister was diagnosed with mild mental challenges. This was evidenced by her inability to comprehend what people were talking about and her paranoia; she was known by the apartment manager where my mother lived, for her angry outbursts.

I felt powerless to assist my mother and sister with moving to more favorable conditions. I was working hard to complete the requirements for my college classes and focusing on taking care of my daughter. I tried to be a responsible daughter by visiting her monthly and bringing her needed items, such as new clothes and food, and giving her money when I could afford to. While visiting my mother, I would suppress the outward tension it caused me—stomachaches, headaches, and sometimes depression. My brother did the best he could to help my mother, considering he was married and raising a family of his own.

By 1994, I started working for a large agency located in Wayne that provided counseling and therapy to adults residing in Wayne County. Shortly after I began working there, I made it my mission to help my mother move out of the unsafe environment she was living in at that time. I noticed a building across the street and inquired whether it was a senior high-rise. Luckily it was, and since this was an emergency situation, my mother was moved to the top of the waitlist.

This was only the second time she lived alone in her entire life. After living over fifty years in Detroit, this entire process proved to be excruciatingly disconcerting for my mother, and she was belligerent to me for months when I visited her. After about six months, she adjusted and over time grew to see that this was a positive change. For many months I visited her daily at lunchtime to listen to her stories about the new friendships she had made. My mother resided in the same apartment for over nineteen years. After moving to her new building, my mother joined a local church and felt accepted there. I want to believe I contributed to helping my mother, through encouragement and determination, in closing the door to many of the mental health challenges she faced when she was young. When one considers her tumultuous past and the severe depression she endured, I feel it was significant that the pastor and congregation reached out to her. They successfully encouraged her to connect with her neighbors, friends, and people living in the community. As more and more time has passed, my mother has become more like a normal parent, and the mental illness that plagued her for so long has faded somewhat. My mother did attend church and that along with learning to relate to others on a deeper level, has significantly helped her in her recovery. Recovery is a process of change and something the person strives toward.

I believe my mother found her purpose late in life. She now feels safe and has learned to develop and maintain close relationships with all of the people surrounding her. She learned that she has people in her life she can trust and go to when she feels overwhelmed.

A NEW WORLD OF POSSIBILITIES

You is kind. You is smart. You is important.

—*Kathryn Stockett*

I have a feeling that my grandfather knew instinctively we all need more than just the basics in life. We need courage, inspiration, balance, harmony, empathy, compassion, respect, discipline, friendship, and spirituality. Robert Frederick Williams had an extraordinary memory, compassion, discipline, empathy and a great sense of humor—he truly walked a path of righteousness for the sake of his family.

My grandfather was a great blessing to me, and I know he always will be. I have learned that as long as each of us has just one person whom we can confide in and who provides us with encouragement and emotional support, we can face the difficulties that confront us as we travel all the roads that lie ahead.

As a small child, I sensed I was here for a purpose. All of the sorrow and times of isolation and challenges ultimately helped to mold me into the person I would become—a person of substance and joy designed by a higher power to overcome difficulties. My goal throughout this book has been to help others see that by combining faith in God with confidence in oneself that they too can face the challenges the world presents them. A new life can be created by focusing on your strengths. Remember, the Bible states, "I will never fail you nor forsake you." Witnessing my grandfather's courage, determination, and perseverance created in me the ability to reach out to others in need and to provide inspiration, comfort, and hope. My goal is to continue to reflect these values and use them daily whether I am counseling a young person or working on a painting. Sometimes we just need to be still, and listen to that inner voice which can stir greatness in us and propel us forward toward achieving our dream.

Tomorrow's challenges and human struggles that we will face in our lives may be difficult and may require great sacrifice. I know if I can hold onto my childhood memories and images of my grandfather, ultimately they remain permanently in my mind and live on in my heart. The birth of the railway occurred in 1828, and just as the rail line and all of its landmarks are indelibly linked; so too was my relationship with my grandfather.

APPENDIX

Help guide

http://www.helpguide.org/mental/depression_signs_types_diagnosis_
treatment.htm

National Alliance on Mental Illness

http://www.nami.org/

National Institute of Mental Health

http://www.nimh.nih.gov/index.shtml

National Library of Medicine: The World's Largest Medical
Library

http://www.ncbi.nlm.nih.gov/pubmedhealth/PMH0001941/

National Suicide Prevention Lifeline

http://www.suicidepreventionlifeline.org/

The US Government's Official Web Portal

http://www.usa.gov/index.shtml

USA National Suicide & Crisis Hotlines

http://suicidehotlines.com/national.html

BIBLIOGRAPHY

Bak, Richard, and Charlie Vincent. *The Corner: A Century of Memories at Michigan and Trumbull.* Chicago: Triumph, 1999. Print.

Barcus, Frank. *Freshwater Fury: Yarns and Reminiscences of the Greatest Storm in Inland Navigation.* Detroit: Wayne State UP, 1960. Print.

Cherry, Kendra. "Hierarchy of Needs: The Five Levels of Maslow's Hierarchy of Needs."*About.com Psychology.* N.P., n.d.http://psychology.about.com/od/theoriesofpersonality/a/hierarchyneeds.htm.

Clark, Alvin C., and Stanislas M. Keenan. *A History of the Wayne County Infirmary, Psychiatric, and General Hospital Complex at Eloise, Michigan, 1832–1982.* Westland MI: Wayne County General Hospital Anniversary Committee, 1982. Print.

Crouch, Tom D., and Peter L. Jakab. *The Wright Brothers and the Invention of the Aerial Age.* Washington, DC: National Geographic, Smithsonian National Air and Space Museum, 2003. Print.

*Diagnostic and Statistical Manual of Mental Disorders: DSM-IV-TR.*Washington, DC: American Psychiatric Association, 2000. Print.

Dukakis, Kitty, and Larry Tye. *Shock: The Healing Power of Electroconvulsive Therapy.* New York: Avery, 2006. Print.

Duncan, Dayton, and Ken Burns. *The National Parks: America's Best Idea: An Illustrated History.* New York: Alfred A. Knopf, 2009. Print.

Ferry, W. Hawkins. *The Buildings of Detroit: A History.* Detroit: Wayne State UP, 1980. Print.

Fort Saint Joseph Museum. Niles, MI

Hauser, Michael, and Marianne Weldon. *Hudson's: Detroit's Legendary Department Store.* Charleston, SC: Arcadia, 2004. Print.

Kincaide, Richard. *The Gods of Olympia Stadium: Legends of the Detroit Red Wings.* Champaign, IL: Sports Pub. LLC, 2003. Print.

Marsh, Nicholas A. *The Michigan Central Railroad: History of the Main Line 1846–1901.* N.P.: 2007. Print.

Mathew, Sanjay J., MD, Jonathan M. Amiel, BS, and Harold A. Sackeim, PhD. "Electroconvulsive Therapy in Treatment-Resistant Depression." *Psychiatry Weekly.*n.d. http://www.psychweekly.com/aspx/Article/articledetail.aspx?articleid=52.

Rh Value Publishing. *Favorite Poems of Emily Dickinson.* New York: Random House Value, 1978. Print.

ːnato M.E., PhD. "The History of ɪpy in Psychiatry." *Brain & Mind.* ʍw.cerebromente.org.br/n04/histo-ɪtm.

rence, and JD. "Psychiatry's Electro ʃhock Treatment: A Crime against ɪ.P. http://www.antipsychiatry.org/.

ɪ. *Counseling Children & Adolescents.* ʹLove Pub., 2009. Print.

CPSIA information can be obtained
at www.ICGtesting.com
Printed in the USA
FSOW03n0217201216
28748FS